T-MAC'S LIFE STORY

T-MAC

authorHOUSE®

AuthorHouse™
1663 Liberty Drive
Bloomington, IN 47403
www.authorhouse.com
Phone: 1 (800) 839-8640

Published by AuthorHouse 04/12/2018

ISBN: 978-1-5462-3530-9 (sc)
ISBN: 978-1-5462-3529-3 (e)

Print information available on the last page.

CHAPTER 1

The senior year of high school in 1986 was such a beautiful thing. I had all the college students asking me lots of questions, "Tmac Kid, what college are you thinking about?", "We can give you a free master's degree, a job, a car, the new 280.z and an apartment! You like that kid? Your job will be to show up on the football field with your teammates." "Sir," I said, "I have not played football with a team or at a school before." "Kid, we will make you a champion! You're fast as hell kid! I'm pretty sure no one can catch you! Here's my card, call me."

My coach saw the college coach hand me his card so he took it out of my hands before I can even look at it. He was angry, "What the hell are you doing handing my boy a business card without asking me?" he said, "Son, go away." It seemed that my coach was mad at that college coach. I couldn't hear what my coach was saying but his hands were going up and down, just like when someone on our team is not running as fast as they could, he would say, "You're bullshit, run it again! You'll run it all until you get it right!" The youngsters' eyes were uncomprehending to what the coach was saying, his hands would be moving faster. I would think, "Maybe he was up late that's why his time is not right, it'snot like him to run that slow." Oh well, it's not me so I shouldn't care much. Nobody knows what my coach was saying to that college coach. Man! All the crap will go down on the schoolyard, yeah! Maybe they will run into each other around the corner. I smiled when I saw coach coming my way, so much thanks for the Good Samaritan. I was thinking what coach was so mad about, but we've seen plenty of those that did not turn out good, right? Thing is, though coach never said much, he ripped apart the college coach' business card, he was acting more like a security than a coach. I was thinking why he did that when coach said, "Son, get warmed up and get ready for the 440 race coming up." "Yes Coach," I said.

My girlfriend, Gigi was there, I looked at her then she blew me a kiss and said, "Baby! Win! Win! Win! For me, baby!" I felt so good, I love her so much and because of her, I win all the time. I was pumped up when coach called me and said, "Now son, it's trouble having her hanging around here, tell her to stop coming here. Do you hear me son? Tell her." I realized that coach wanted Gigi out of my life right away. I figured maybe coach would like her so I told him she's the reason why I win all the time, maybe it's stupid, but I don't know. I guess I was in love with the way she looked at me. She knew that something is wrong by the crazy look I had on my face. "Baby, is something wrong?" Gigi said, looking sharply at my coach. Deep inside, I was saying, "This is not right, Coach! I know she can make me happy", but instead, I said, "I'm just happy, you're here with me". I was laughing but my eyes glittered with pain that I'm trying to hide. I know that she came a long way from Long Beach to Las Vegas just to see me win these races.

The weather in Vegas was cold and windy, the wind was blowing fast, and it seemed like it was snowing in Las Vegas that day. Cumulonimbus clouds in the sky, unthinkable cold weather, and a total contempt for human life; it was the most menacing day of my life. The disturbing question is: WHY? Coach asked me why I was looking at the love of my life sitting there, with a cold to death look on her face. I guess everyone was cold but me, my blood was boiling hot, I was warming up, moving faster and faster so coach told me to slow it down. He said, "You are warming up, not racing, son". I kept going faster and faster like a mad man, I mean mad with the question "Why? Why coach? She's my girlfriend?!"

Then I heard coach said, "Boy, it's time to go." I was still on the track, you can see the gray steam coming off my body. I took off my uniform and there was more steam coming off me. I could hear people in the stands murmuring something like, "He's a ghost! Look at him, man!" Well, apparently not, I thought, maybe someone did think I was a ghost staring a gun shot. I thought, it's Flash Gordon today baby! I cut through the high wind like I was a knife. Two years of coaching meant nothing to me right now, I ran the first 220 in 23 seconds and roll the other 220 on into the finish line. I ran like I was running the 100 yard dash, like a car on a freeway getting out of the way of traffic, all I remember was snagging the first line. It was an interesting reaction from everyone; my coach, the officials and the people in the stands maybe it has something to do with my running time, it was unbelievable. They were like prize fighters' battered faces looking at their watches, I didn't know the exact time I ran, but they said that the wind pushed me, who knows? The world's fastest kid or man, no one came close to Flash Gordon. No, they just took it away. I won, but Gigi wouldn't know. She would always say, "You know who that is out there? My hero!" and would toss me flying kisses.

The track was my playground, I made eyebrows rise on the track field. All eyes were on me when we go to other schools on a track field trip, I'm always a hero in all schools. I enjoyed being the center of attention, but the time I lost touch and trust in my coach was when he told Gigi to stop coming to my track meet. They had a conflict and both of them drifted away. When I asked them what happened, they would say nothing. Gigi was always cheerful and optimistic, it was probably why she stroked out holding it all inside. "I don't want to make you mad, T-Mac." Gigi said. She sounded worried then it all came out, "I thought you were a regular guy partying and chasing girls. You think you're smarter than me, huh? I thought you were different T-Mac. I loved you only!" I was at a red light. When my life seemed happy, there will always something to fuck it up. I knew it was about what coach did.

I could feel too much pain. She bit her lower lip and said, "I don't love you anymore!" I hadn't heard nor seen her since. I freaked out. I called her but she won't pick up. She knew it was me but she didn't pay me any attention, now I lost touch of her. When I went to her apartment, an old lady said, "Baby, they moved two and half months ago." I asked the lady if she knows where they move to but she said, "We were never close like that, baby. You are a very good-looking young man." She smiled and said, "What's your name boy?"

"T-Mac, Ma'am!" I said.

"On the contrary," she said, "she always talked about you. She was a very outgoing girl more than her mother." Gigi is a very beautiful girl, my heart fuzzed about remembering how beautiful she was. I lost touch of myself. I was the guy you notice when you enter a class room, just smarter. I always get A's even without working hard. "The old lady said she would call you, give her time and have some faith" she said. She might know the truth but all I can do was think that maybe we were never close, and there were more tears. I just drifted away from coach and my teammates on the track field and my class mates would say things to me that was hard to believe. Like the track team said, they were going to fuck me up and the girls would get you in trouble and kick your ass! I remained serious and smart. I thought I was brilliant from one class to the other.

I'm a good fighter, growing up in the project you have to fight or get beaten up or get your money or shoes taken. My Dad will always say "There is no punk living in this house!" you grow up fast in the projects. The only thing I can think of is Dad had gotten politically conservative. There is real law-and- order in his house and he also said "Not me!" which refers to me. Dad calls me "Not me" because when I was three or so, I always said, "Not me, Dad", to not get in trouble. Well, a good way of saying it instead of "You are a liar!" to finish up things, maybe I was rebelling "Well, not me!" Mom was heavily into education of her sons and the kingdom hall. Yes, my Mom was a Jehovah's Witness. I am sure that we share her interest in providing reading materials for all her sons, the most important thing is, "Love for Jehovah, our God", and for this reason I was not going to fight the track team, I guess I am a Ghost. I remember back at that track meet in Las Vegas, someone said "he looks like a ghost!". I was convinced I'll outsmart them all. When the school bell rang for the next period, I am always in my classroom so fast that the teacher made me the student teacher's aide. Sitting here thinking, "God, help me stay out of trouble". Keeping my activities to myself, my love for running is still unbeatable and just because I was mad at coach, I didn't stop to run on my own, I win for myself. I thought that I see faces of my love ones' ghost faces in the stands at my track meet and now it's Gigi's, she is always on my mind when I run on the Beach sand, I run so fast to catch her but she was way faster, then she's gone.

My knee wiped out. I fell right on my face, ate sand and my hands hit the sand then I thought, "Why, Gigi why?" It was like I was hearing her thoughts laughing at me, "I thought you were different, T-Mac. I don't love you anymore!" It kept running in my mind over and over again. Could I change the fact that I lost the two important things in my life? My relationship with Gigi and my passion for running. How should I spend my time? How should I enjoy life? What should I do to help me feel better? How can I change what has happened?

My two unbeatable loves. Where are my friends? Are they really my friends? As long as I keep on winning races, they are friends. One fact about me as a little boy was I always had a day dream that I can fly. I got off the sand laughing, then it all came to me! I realized I was immature to this teenage stuff like school, sports and girls, I was not as intellectual as I thought I was, but that's not exactly what came to my mind when you say intellectual, right? It's been months since I have not put on any physical harm to anyone on the track team or them on me. All my classmates would have loved to see some actions. Someone will get their ass kicked in class if we had free time. So I picked up a book with a title, "Choosing good health to make time pass" I opened it up, and right there it said, "Emotional Health" I thought, "Will this teach you how to live with your feelings?"

Good emotional health means that you have good feelings about yourself. Knowing how to make wise decisions helps you have good emotional health. "That's me", I said. I kept on reading social health so I would know better how to get along with others. Good social health means you try to get along with your family and friends, and you care about helping others, that's my mom. She kept on telling this to us all the time so the book would be a great help to me.

I was starting to feel good about being sad and angry, thinking about studying and not running my mouth like some of my class mates. I made a wise decision to reach wellness. There were two or three choices in solving my problem so I thought about my choices. I could go back to P.E. class with coach, I could join back on the track team or to stay with the job that I have. I went to school for half a day, and worked for J&G construction for the other half. I loved my job and I enjoyed being with friends on the track team but I don't want to risk my family.

We lived in the projects, we had no money or food and sometimes we ate plain baked potato or French fries for dinner and French fries was "O.D.R" in our house half of the time. We would not have cooking oil so we usually just ate plain baked potato. On French fries days, it was always a fight who would get to the table first. You want ketchup for your fries in our house? Huh! The only ketchup you get is if you take too many fries off the plate and you get busted in the nose. There were only a few to go around. I would always dream about butter cream cakes, cookies, whole milk and ice cream. My little brother who was sleeping on top of the bunk bed would slap me and tell me to stop talking in my sleep because it makes him hungry hearing all the sweet and fatty snacks. I would play the big brother role and say, "Take your little butt back to sleep before I beat you up!" And he would pass gas and say "you eat that" then we laugh. We were not rich and did not live in Beverly Hills but we were one big, happy, poor family and we always have a good time.

I'm having a day dream again, but thank God it's not about flying but about the good old days. I thought about earning some money to get things that we need at home and all extra things, I had to make the right decision. I looked up and put the book down when I saw Coach in my Math class, talking to my teacher who's looking at me the whole time they were talking. "T-Mac!" he called. I haven't decided on anything yet because anything I tell coach will go straight to the track team and I don't want a high-powered coach to know at this point that I am grieving.

"T-Mac, did you hear me?"

"Yes ma'am!" Both of them looked at me.

"Your coach would like to see you outside, okay?" she said. Coach said, "Thanks a lot"

"No problem", she said and flashed an abrupt smile. She speaks in a soft voice most of the time but I never pay attention to her. She had a little makeup to add depth to her eyes but she doesn't need that anymore. She had very long hair, thin hands with strong fingers that squeezed mine for a second. Her eyes flew back to coach and said, "Coach is waiting for you"

"Oh yeah", I said. "What's up, Coach?"

He gave me the eagle eye look, but I smiled. You probably never heard a sullied speech, most of the time they're bullshit speech, and I knew that coach was going to lay down one on me, "What's up is," coach said, "Son, are you that egotistical? I'm not trying to get between your relationship with Gigi!" I was thinking that coach was underestimating me and this was no way to win at black jack. Eventually he said, "You do not need a relationship yet. What can you do for her now? Nothing, son! What is she doing for you? Nothing! What the hell, boy? You live in a project, there is no future there! An alley full of drugs and alcoholic people with no plan or education or any long term goals. They will die there or get killed!

Is that the neighborhood that you want, son? You can help your family, get them out of the project. College is the key or you will be working at McDonalds or be in prison for life, there will be transsexuals there! I know you don't want that project life, son." I felt a little out of balance when I heard all that, when he said those to me, he was eating a forkful of pie. I was thinking of my dream to get out off the ghetto. "I learned you couldn't prepare for anything well hmm..." coach said. "Life's full of new experiences, go see the world son! I have college connections! It's up to you to have long term goals, it's your life at hand. I'll see you on the track field". "Yes coach," I said. He smiled again and shook his head and said it was good getting his sugar rush with that doughnut head, he's black leather, not coach leather. Laughing hard, he joked "Well, life's full of new experiences," and the only thing I can thought of was, he's right!

Gigi is gone, too. But one day, she'll see me on T.V. and she will come back to me. She has hypertension but she never took care of it. She was only sixteen but maybe she's the lucky one who does not have to know that I was divorced and loved only her. It's my dark side, so I'm bearing all this alone. The last thing I would have thought is that coach set me up, who knows? I was in the locker room and I can see coach talking to three of my teammates. I was putting books in my locker (It developed an us-them-thing fight for the team) they told him why they were beating me up. It was so public, right in front of all those people and coach like they were saying "screw you" to the world. No one expected me to join the track team after all that existential stuff, the meaninglessness of life. I felt coach crossed me and he's so unpredictable. I owed it to my parents and Gigi to move out of the project and be stable, so I'm going to prove that I'm a team player. I went to the bathroom and changed my clothes, whatever the reason, I never knew.

They were pretty cool about it. I don't think they really ever understood me, but I never saw them put me down or made fun of me. Running was my passion and no one can stop me. It was funny to see the look on their faces when I walked down that track eating an apple. Each one of them had a look of disbelief that I was back! I felt so strange, like who's bad! "I'm in your establishment!" I felt like saying, "I'm not wiping my eyes with some tissue, I come out here to kick some ass, this is my playground!" I guess all eyes were on me. I had something completely different in mind, only I knew about. I can hear the girls saying, "I thought he stopped hanging out with us, my best friend said, he always preferred to be by himself and do his own thing. Now that I think about it, he always kept his life private". I can hear one of my teammate and coach railing about something. "He hasn't been to practice in a long time coach", he said "like you said coach, missing one day of practice is like missing a week of practice, right?" I remembered coach said, "I knew the reason for that, he was all up for it. Now, he's the fastest on the team!" So now, I'm back. I take his spot to fix things fast with coach, he must have said that he can beat me, and he was pretty cold. I was warmed up and stretching and no one knows that I have been exercising on my own at the beach and my muscles were stronger. I felt that I had built three physical fitness exercises on the sand, although Gigi kicked my ass in my mind. I felt more endurance, strength, and flexibility in my legs. I felt like running. I just ignored them all, or at least I thought so.

"Anything from love to hate can follow", coach said before I could get to the track field. I knew what coach was going to say before he said it. I knew his name tag was still pinned to be the King. "Well son", coach said, "it's like this, he thinks you're not as good as you used to be". The door opened and he got a face full of smile, coach put it in a nice way. "But kick my ass on the track in the 440 race, okay?" I said. Any other relatives besides V.I.P here who want some? Write down the appointment. "I'll call you, maybe around ten in the morning? Hello! Hello! Who's on the line?" I really miss them more than I thought, right after that, I looked around with blank stares and eyes everywhere, coach shook his head. Is it a possibility that he's right? Have I been gone too long and will soon find myself ensnared in one of the darkest, most menacing days of my life? If he win! I'm in a mind though alone, to expose the unthinkable and I wished for it to go away just disappear. I lost my self-righteousness, my thrill and specially the love for running, and what for? Gigi still hadn't called. Maybe she'd decided that only she would understand what coach had done and would have wanted me to drop out? And on some level that didn't bother me because coach was right. Real answers were often unobtainable. Just before I stepped onto the track, I looked up in the stands where Gigi always sat with her clean pretty face buttered by the sun. I saw a picture of happiness. No puffed ghost face of her this time, but the thoughts remained. That's right! I'm here, showing off, could this have been making a statement? "Pretty bizarre", I said to myself. I thought of Gigi, she would have said "You know how it is out here? My hero!", blowing me a kiss and saying "Baby, win, win, win!" No one seconded the motion. Coach would say, "Set... Go!" I had so much energy, he felt like he met his self execution! Drained his and refilled mine against no rule, I said, "But they know me here, this is my playground where I made you ate my dust, where the wind carries me away. I'll be at the finish line before the dust smoke dissolves in your face, eat my dust!" It wasn't a matter of losing or winning but breaking off some major teammate relationship. The training period was limited, we needed to learn and go out into this big bad world. No! I have to win back my self-righteousness and my thrill for running. When I crossed the finish line, coach harrumphed and turned away and resumed looking at his watch.

Two years of knowing coach Leather, and I have never seen him run before off the track field and not come back that way. We all hanged out and coach disappeared. One of the girls said, "Why did coach leave?" Mr. M.V.P himself answered, "Jesus! Are you retarded or something? And to me, they were a perfect match. We laughed and left for home. At home, I thought about what coach told me. Our home is known as the gang's hangout. In the project, you can hear gunshots, see drugs sold in the sidewalks, the usual alcohol bottles on the ground, and a crack head named Silky always asking for money looking fucked up and nasty looking. He has a "Slick Rick" smile because he was always running his mouth a mile a minute for you if you hook up with him. If you stand there long, he will talk you out of your money. He thought he's a pimp, the project thug! He called his girlfriend," the hoe, what a big pussy, bitch and the next door neighbor's wife" acting like she cannot comprehend. When a ghetto hoe asked if she's fucking her man, I can hear her talking to her friend when they left, "Girl, don't say nothing to my husband. That Hoe is lying and will make my husband upset or anything", her friend would say "Mmm... Girl, you know those bitches are haters, that's why I just can't get along with those ghetto hoes, ha!ha!ha!" That's right, my project life! She knew that if he found out that shit, he'd kick her ass. I'm laying in bed thinking about this crazy day and why Coach left us on the track, he was so unhappy. That's not coach's behavior. What could it be? Well, I had a successful day. If you had smoke detectors today on the track, it would tell you to leave the track because it's on fire! My shoes were flaming, they quickly caught fire and smoke of dust, I made his ass "eat my dust!" "Who called 911?" It's just a fire drill! (Choking) choking...

I was in bed still thinking about all this when I heard a gunshot, like always. Things got to the point where only blood can bring the police out and even then, not with much enthusiasm. Exactly no quick protection. I thought, "Oh, I'm getting sleepy I think I will go see coach tomorrow." In the hallway at school, two geeks looked at me, so I wondered about that high IQ group. I shook my head and thought, "Hell, I hope college won't be like that." Sitting by the library door, I remembered something my father once told me. He was an alcoholic professor, a physical ghetto anthropologist. He did research on trying to figure out which comes first, the bottle or the alcohol. But them geeks, library or classroom, dammit! All of us retarded know it open up after second period. I just promise that if I stand around a memo, you'll read about it.

"What's up, Coach? I come to ask you about yesterday. I thought I ran a good time, what was it coach?" The way coach looked at me was like he already had a feeling in his gut that I would ask about my running time. Coach said, "What kind of equipment you have at home son?" I said, "Coach, I have no equipment at my house", so coach said, "Well, son you been doing something. Are you still working for G&J construction?" "Well, coach" I said, "we do not have that much work lately coach but I still work there. When work picks up, I'll be back to work." "I see", coach said "what is your phone number at work son?" I gave it to coach, and he said, "Son, you need to quit that job because it wore you down son." I listened to him going on and on. I felt heartbroken and sad for Gigi and then now he wanted me to quit my other job. Coach was crazy, I thought that he was losing his mind. I didn't move nor speak. Images of coach were flashing in my head as though there was a projector there, thinking that sports is nothing like I remember growing up.

"Nothing! one, two, three, nothing!" I felt like I just died and someone stopped my breathing, my eyes rolled up into my head, someone held open my mouth and breathed into it "nothing one, two, three, nothing, one two, three, nothing". I turned ghostly gray, I looked at coach but my mind was a million miles away, thinking he was not as young as he might think he is. Would coach mind if I asked what he does in his spare time? But I called it dirt. Coach would not give me my running time without being over aggressive, he was always low- key but straightforward. Although he is in a captain-of-a-soccer- team way, he's a top investigator in his office about my business. I was thinking that this is the United States of America, you can be all the shit you want. Coach was crazy, I'm keeping my job. He destroyed my relationship with Gigi and stolen her heart away from me, without permission. Everything unfolds in perfect sequence like a thoroughbred under the whip. I don't go for much of what coach was saying, "work out equipment or my job draining me". Maybe it's the fact that on the sand on the beach, it's just me and myself in my head, and no one else needs to know!

`The beach was my get away from it all, I stepped unsteadily onto a lovely stretch of fine sand, the power of beauty is as absurd as it is undeniable, like a memory from a previous life. For some reason, the beach was my home. Unfortunately, when they dropped back half way along the track they were on their last position. The other team had stopped crying but I cannot see because of the dust on one side of the end zone. "Dana, who won?" I know Gigi whispered but that wasn't the best part. The best part was the kiss I gave Gigi, I was so happy. I could feel it, I don't care what anyone said, and it never got any better than that. The whole time I was having a day dream in my class but my teacher woke me up at the last instant of getting a kiss. "Man!" I was about to say the words, "I love you" to her. I started to cry and once I got started I couldn't stop for ten minutes, then I got so cold, my teeth chattered.

I couldn't believe I was on the beach with Gigi. I was never going to see her again, and now here I am sitting in class thinking of ways to clean up this nasty mess coach gave me. My teacher startled me from a dream in which I was trying to save Gigi's heart. I could still hear the deep smack kiss. I remembered the very first time I saw her at a bus stop and we exchanged phone numbers. I was in the driveway looking at a beautiful girl that made my heart fuzzy because of her pretty face. I was about to fall out when she gave me her number. I was the MAC, I got a hold of myself as I was saying and Gigi cross examined me to make sure that I don't have a girlfriend. "Of course not" I said, perhaps she thought that the sooner we got our ex's out, the better. My testimony was the truth, for a change,

I was hoping I did not sound nervous, but I drew a deep breath, but upon big consideration I did not experience on soul-searching. I felt close to her, I realized what I felt for her, and she was speechless. I couldn't believe what I'd just heard, she said, she'd call me and I had to admit that she looked as good as ever! Whatever the exact tragic circumstances that coach said to her, I still loved Gigi. Now I appreciate for those of you who get to stop at a red light, it's going green again and you go on. You, who have stayed with me this far, there's nothing too surprising about this romantic love that developed, you probably saw it coming! But I didn't. The call, "Hello?" "Yes, this is me!" I was at home watching T.V. when the phone rang. It was my favorite cartoons show "Bugs Bunny and the Turtle." The turtle always beats the rabbit! From that day on my nick name was Turtle. I loved that turtle, he always outsmarted the rabbit, that would be coach and me.

I was thinking, on that track I'm going to outsmart them all because I'm the turtle. Hey! I like it "Turtle! Yes that's me, ha, ha, ha!" Bugs bunny was so funny, he reminded me of some people on a different track team. He took off super fast but ran out of gas before the first line, coach call it the "monkey jump on your back". I love this cartoons show, and now I'm on the phone with my Boss, "Yes sir", I said, and Mr. Gregory said, "I played sport in High school young man and it is a total commitment with no reserve, no retreat and no regrets. Give a man a dollar and you cheer his heart. Give him a dream, and you challenge his heart. Now young man I'm not firing you, because you are one of my excellent workers. When the track season is over you can come back, T-Mac. Hey! I hear you are pretty good, Coach Leather told me something about you and not to tell you. Hell! Son you are that bad huh! You go for it son! I wish I kept my dream to be a baseball player! You owe it to yourself first and your teammates. You'll thank coach and me later T-Mac, when you make it big. Remember me, son okay?" "Yes sir!" I said for some reason.

I found myself thinking, about me being a proactive, but I have no money right now. I was thinking of getting mad when my little brother was asking something. I want off of him, "Anthony! I take enough shit in this life without having to take more from you. Get the hell out of here! Get lost!" and Anthony said sarcastically, "You are a cry baby because you are a little punk over Gigi. I love Gigi, Gigi!" I jumped up out of my chair stuck his face in mine, grabbed his shirt, and pushed him hard against the wall and said, "I should kick your little ass right now, you piece of shit!" He kicked me right in the balls, I let him go and he ran so fast. I could not believe my little brother had wheels like that. All I could do was smile. I knew he does not have the ability to back up his words, but the way I felt, maybe that wasn't the best day to get in the ring with my baby brother. I released my mind and sat down holding my balls in my hand, thinking about shit. My face hardened. Coach just doesn't leave me alone," if you wanted one reason, I got three" Now go away! It sounded pretty good to me when I was thinking that bullshit that my boss and coach were saying but it was all total crap. "Trust me on this one, go for your dream", I will thank them later? What am I missing here? Hell my dream. I'm laughing. My dreams are cream cakes, cookies, whole milk and ice cream, like my little brother said, "stop dreaming, you make me hungry".

Yes, that was the good old days, the love of family, always laughing. I remembered Anthon pass gas, and said, "Eat that gas!" Now, he fucked me up! My balls are still hurting. I saw that look that crossed his face. I owe him an apology tonight. I almost gave him a heart attack or at least a broken heart. I love my little brother, sometimes they get on your nerves but that's what family does. Like my older brother Keith said, we both get on his nerves when he is in his room playing music. He still thinks he's a DJ, it's an honest business in a way. I'm proud of my older brother because young teenagers his age in the project are selling dope, but my older brother has a dream to be a star, a big music producer. I always believed he will become one. I'm thinking about my long term goals, an architect when I go to college. I am the best in my drafting class, my teacher Mr. Finnly always tells me that I have skills for drafting. I spend my lunch time in the drafting class, I stop going to the gym. I began to love architect drafting. Mr. Finnly told me about this R.O.P Art fair coming up and to read this architect book and pick a project out of it to put in the fair. "I loved this beach house", I said. It was my dream house, I will build a hexagon beach house that looks like a stop sign. When life seems to be at a red light, when you're at a stop sign, it always goes green so you can get to your goals. Reminds me of something Jesus said that a solid foundation is if someone asks you to walk a mile, do not just not walk a mile but walk an extra mile. And I'm going to remain loyal, I alone as a black man bears that designation to go an extra mile.

Months pass, we were kicking ass in the track field. Yes, we were scalping heads. "Who, who, who! The Apache is coming for you!" Well, we were all big chiefs, we earned our heads scalping it was like first plays after first plays. Our stands got packed with schoolmates. It was all the school spirit doing the Indian dance on the field. We were the warriors, the big chiefs going after our victims. The Apache was making a name for ourselves. L.A. times had us in the page, we were the team that people from the streets were coming for in Centennial High School in Compton, and we were. In the show, all the school class clowns were getting there clowning on. One was talking like he's Howard Coldcell, the sports announcer saying, "Here we are at Centennial High School where you can say, look at that monkey run, without getting in trouble! Look at the kid better known as "eat my Dust", who calls himself "Turtle"! But ladies and gentlemen, he's not running against the silly rabbit, turtle have to outsmart the fox!" It was laughter all through the stands, I felt like a star, people called me all kind names, good nicknames, something to do with "fast". I know you have your name for me too, "run forest run!" We kicked ass all season long when the dust clouds the air and you wonder where your hair is at. When you ask one of them Apache, they will tell you "where it's at, who, who, who!"

My life is a traffic light, it stops and goes all the time. When you are at a green light, life is good making that money, when that light change yellow some people give up on there long term goals thinking it will change green again, but not knowing that they are at a red light. They were doing so badly. I guess you knew it was that damn traffic light!

That day is the day of elimination of schools that were trying to go to the C.I.F meet. Just outside were Compton cable T.V. truck and the camera man on top filming the track meet. No one was more surprised by the size and intensity of the outpouring than I. All of our fans were cheering for us. I always assumed I will be on T.V. one day. I've had too many happy occasions, but not like that one. I looked into the stands of people, whether God in heaven chooses that you and I were going to get to the bottom of this, I were dry-eyed that evening at least to me I was, and I saw her in the front row, hand on her knee. Both of us knew that a look had been made, she was dressed in old blue jeans and a pink T-shirt, her lips looked so soft, her eyes weren't just beautiful but they showed off how pretty her face is. I guess I knew it all well, I could see by the way she looked at me that she was still hurting, no sparkle in her eyes, not like the Gigi I knew. I got up from stretching my legs and went to the stands. Gigi said, "I thought you might be here". "I called your house a bunch of times Gigi" I said. "They really like you T-Mac, don't they?" Gigi said, and snuck a look at my friends. All the people in the stands were trying to get my attention calling me all the names in the book. Gigi said, "I'll go if you want me to. Really, T-Mac, I just wanted to make sure you were okay. Are you?" "Nope! That's why I'm glad you're here". I tried to lean in and kiss her, but she leaned back and it crushed my heart. I still couldn't believe that she's here, and the fact that the two of us were together. She was so beautiful, my coach and friends on the team hadn't given her a chance yet, but they will come around once they got to know her. I figured Gigi still loved me, she was hurting right now that's why she refused the kiss, so I told her "After the track meet, I would like to see you Gigi", she just sat there with a cool but dark look in her face, I said to myself, "what was that all about?" For some reason, that look was the last look she gave me the last time I saw her. I found myself thinking about that, she bit her lower lip the same way the last time she said, "I don't love you any more".

My thoughts were suddenly shattered by loud crash voices of people directly overhead. What the hell? Something must have happened, I turn around and the track meet has started, and I barely said the last few words. I started getting lightheaded, the kind you get only after doing something really hard. I don't care what anyone thought about me, I told Gigi I love her. It never gets any better than that, I have been holding on to those delicate matters for so long and with such efficiency, she was lied to by coach. Maybe she thought that I was still partying and chasing girls and that I'm no different than a player. Somehow, someway I had to prove to her that I'm not! Coach called me, "What up! Coach?", he said, "You over there running your mouth son? This is the big day of elimination and this school is not like the others in the 2A lead, they have guys that will give you a race for your money so there's no playing out here today. Give it your best and kick some ass okay son? Get warm up!". Coach was giving me his pump up speech, the green light special, get your money and that's what I was going to do without a doubt. Although Gigi had dampened my enthusiasm to win, it was always her pumping me up before I run my race. When I looked up at her sitting there, her spirit seemed dead, not the spirit I once knew blowing me a kiss and saying "baby win, win, win, for me baby!"

I felt so hurt, but I had no idea how hurt could I be. Like Dad always said, it's better to be surprised than disappointed. I'm at a yellow light, I can go for it or stop! For the first time in my life, I was in love. I was singing a song in my mind, "Going to the finish line, Baby, do you want to go? I'm going to the finish line, Baby, do you want to go?" When I heard the officials say "Runners! On your march, get set, go!" But go is starter gunshot, I was up about as fast as I went down. At the finish line, there were interview after interview for all the winners. I can hear girls yelling to me from the stands, saying, "Be my boyfriend, you sexy fine ass." "Sexy body, I'll eat you up", this time names that had nothing to do with running. It was plain to see that the girls were coming for me. I looked where Gigi was seated but she vanished from sight, she had moved so fast like she just saw a ghost. So I ran over there and asked my friends and classmates if they have seen her, "The girl that was sitting right here!", I yelled. By the time I maneuvered around them, I still didn't see her, I turned and dashed back out the front rows of seats when I heard my name, "Hey Turtle!", she keeps calling me turtle. I said, "Not now, Michelle, I'm looking for...", she cut me off, "You are looking for that white bitch, huh?" I was thinking this couldn't be happening with a look of disbelief on my face, and Michelle said, "Her name is Gigi or something like that Turtle?" "Yeah, Yeah, Michelle!" I said, eyes rolled up into my head to keep me from crying and breathed deeply. "But I was pretty sure that whatever relationship Gigi and I had, is now pretty much over", I said to Michelle. "She is not white, she is mix black and white because her mom is white but her Dad is black, okay? So stop calling her a white bitch Michelle!". "Well, to me", Michelle said, "Nigga, the bitch looks white to me. She told me to give you this". I looked at the letter in Michelle's hand, I thanked her for giving it to me. She said, "Huh, I saw your ass running up and down the steps. Hell! I said to myself I better give this Nigga this letter before his ass falls and hurt his back. Hell Nigga they need your ass to win!", we laughed. I slightly opened the letter, after Michelle walk off laughing, talking shit about me like always. I knew she loved me as a friend, I do too. I sat down and opened the letter, I pushed my way through the crowd of people, all of them giving me props about my run, shaking hands and all new girls I have not seen before handing me their phone numbers. I said, "no, thank you, I have a girlfriend". I can hear her scream. He touch my hand, I smiled and just kept going. I felt like a star on T.V. today and I'm on my interview, when I reached the locker room, I pushed against the door, met some of my teammates and high five some of them. I wriggled through and turne right, and set out across the main floor right to my locker, sat down on the wood bench and opened up Gigi's letter that I had in my left hand to read it again. When I reached the end of the letter, it was good to be reminded of why Gigi have not called and why she ignored all my questions today. I xz'remembered thinking that she's the lucky one not having to know I am still single and only maintained love for her. I realized it was both of us on the dark side, she cannot bear it alone, she liked to know where she stand in my life. Man, a thousand girls and the only lucky girl I love would be the one that I take to the prom. I feel something telling me that we are just alike. I have to take first plays when I'm on that track. If I come in second or third, I feel like a zero, the way Gigi feels if she cannot come first. The idea who is number one, and all them thousand of girls are powerless to her, the others get dismissed. I stood there immobile, but as I struggled to come up with the right response to her letter, because if I tell her the truth she will think I'm a lying playboy to get what I want. I guess her love, which is the truth. But for Gigi, it is not only her but a new girlfriend! She'd like to see who she lost me to, to call her and tell her who I'm going to the prom with. I had no idea who to say, but I want to ask her to go as my date. She will feel that she wins number one, I felt that I just ran a red light, and hope I do not get caught. If I may say so myself, it is so persuasive but it will work even though I felt okay about my day on TV and Gigi, as a matter of fact, we kicked there ass out there today.

I get dress and headed to the project, I was immediately at home at last, "Hey mom!" "Boy, aren't you going to eat?" Mom said," I'm not all that hungry", I said. I felt I was on top of the world. Looking at my little brother unwrapped a chicken sandwich on twelve-grain, it was a big sandwich for such a slender boy like my brother, and Mom knew it, too. I would always eat the left over on my brother's plate, we were poor but today there was no starvation in our house that the best thing mom put on my plate! I stepped out to hear what she's going to say right on the phone, I called the number Gigi put down to call, it was just ringing then someone picked up, my heart started beating fast although there was no response. I said,

"Hello!" I recognized Gigi's mother's voice,

"Who's this?"

"Tmac Ma'am", I said.

"Tmac! I cannot believe this!", she realized the phone call has something to do with Gigi,

"Tmac", she said, "Baby, Gigi is not home. I'll tell her you called".

The first thing I could think of was,

"I'm calling for you Ma'am!" "For me?" she said,

"Yes Ma'am",

"You said your name is T-Mac, the only T-Mac I know is Gigi's exboyfriend", "Yes Ma'am, that's me!"

"How did you get my number T-Mac?" she said.

"Gigi told me she was going to her friend's house, some girl she go to school with. But you said, you wanted to talk to me T-Mac, about what?"

"Yes Ma'am, I want to ask if I can take Gigi to the prom", her voice switched like it was trouble to answer my question, she said, "Have you asked Gigi that T-Mac?"

"No Ma'am, I was thinking the right thing to do is ask you first", she showed no response for a long time. "Okay, there's a chance Gigi might say no, and I tell you yes. It's all right by me but it's up to her."

"Thank you Ma'am, can you tell her for me? Have her call me, my number is..."

The two of us fell into an enthusiastic discussion about the prom and Gigi. I hope her mom's intention and efforts will resolve this situation as quickly as possible. Today my face seems to have broken into a million shimmering pieces looking for Gigi after the track meet. That Michelle got her clowning on, I was flying back and forth over every square inch of the stands. Gigi looked more beautiful than I have ever seen. I was sitting here afraid to move, waiting for the frightening phone call from Gigi. I always assumed Gigi's mom unappreciated my call, I hope that wasn't the case. I was playing music, the song had a lovely hooky sound. I don't know the name of the song or who sang it, but it tears up my eyes and keeps running over and over in my mind, something like, "No roses, no candle light, no slow dance Baaabbbyyy, maybe we can try that just the way it is. Maybe we can try again, try, maybe we can try again, no romance, maybe that's just the way it is…" After hearing that song, all that thought made me think I'm brilliant. Yes! I learned that I cannot prepare for a thing, life is full of new experiences. That song is right, Gigi and I have a relationship like that, come to think about it, no romance, it was all about me. I mean, we never went out, no movies, no nothing, only my track meet. Our relationship was built around the track field, at my track practice all the time, she was there more than some of my teammate, and she never missed a practice or track meet. Our relationship was all about me, Gigi loved me, she supports me 100% in running. I see now why coach said, "Son, now it's trouble having her hanging around here", and the way Gigi feels knowing that she is the one who deserves to have a romantic night at the prom, to get it all in one, roses, a candlelit dinner, and a slow dance. Man! That's right, maybe that's just the way it is, maybe she is M.V.P. I will tell her I appreciated her for the support and all the time she gave me the strength to win and the fact that I had no money to take her out somewhere romantic and I owe her that.

Yes! I think that should make it really easy for me. I hope she will go for it, I wouldn't call Gigi back today either, I walked to the kitchen, got my chicken sandwich and went to my bedroom and left the door half open so I can hear if the phone rings. I was lying in bed eating my sandwich, thinking about my day. Man! I'm on TV, I hope I get to see myself. Who do I know that have Compton cable at their house? No one I knew in these projects. Well, I better read my Architect book because Mr Finnly asked me to put my drawing in the fair, it's coming up pretty good. I'm thinking about making a replica model of my dream house, I will ask my teacher Mr. Finnly if I can. It would be nice to actually see my dream house and not just on some rice paper, to make the blue print come out good. I hate that blue print machine, the smell of amonia will make the whole class light up. Man that's the only thing I hate about my drafting class, in those days, I just wanted some fresh air.

I was getting tired of reading and my mouth went dry, but I had no idea how tired I was. Well, today was a good day after all, I think I got Gigi back. At worse, we can be friends and she can see for herself that I'm not like what coach said,that I was a player. Now, at least I can call her to hear the sound of her voice and not to have to memorize it. I was about to feel hurt not about me losing Gigi or anything, it's that, I don't really know anything about Gigi. I mean, the dreams of her heart, her feelings, our relationship was always build up around my dreams, more than anything else. I knew I want to make her happier than she was before, and give her all the things her heart truly deserves. But what does she love, her likes and dislikes, have I been selfish? The sun was spilling out over the window, right in my face. I jump up and no one was in the house, today mom goes out to field service, you know what I'm talking about. Don't act like no Jehovah's witnesses ever knocked on your door before. If we don't know where you at, we will find you. Are you smiling? I hope so, because you are not one of them, I have to kick your butt, slamming the door on my face, or say out loud "We are not home!". Man I think people don't want to hear the truth. Well, I better take my bus to school. Why have Gigi not called me? I hope her mom told her. Well, I will see her after school today, she goes to a private all girls school called "Regina Kelly", so as soon as I get home she will be at the top of the list to call, you know, oppurtunity knocks. It's the new American dream. "To be all you can be", coach pointed out only among some. "The first aspect of leadership I learned during my seventeen years of life is, you lead by example and in Los Angeles, you will not change people's minds by arguing with them in there hood or project, you just shut up,and you will live long", old "G" said. Among some, yes, the hood pointed out only among some. "Now," I say, "you disagree with someone and you're accused of hating whatever minority they happen to belong to, and you two are opposite sets. Hell, it is a new world. I guess what we need are electronic earplugs, if we don't hear what we don't like, we don't run the risk of getting killed or being politically incorrect". The old minds don't choose them. Yeah, well I'm from the project, we have no road model, only a doggy-dog world. Sooner or later, it all comes around to that. The strong survives. I know the feeling because when I'm on that track field, I take no hostages. It's like I have the power and they are my enemies, like a power failure, which takes your computer data with it. That's why I'm the boss and you are not. You see, the most desirable things always fade away; dreams, youth and passion. Like listening to music, no matter how much you like it you still have to rewind it, the beautiful ugliness of it all. Yes! I rely on earplugs for peace of mind. That takes me right to a better place, when life sits at a red light, when your heart melts for love.

I was having a hard time today concentrating in class, all I can think of is Gigi and why she hasn't called me back yet, or maybe she has but I was asleep and no one bothered to wake me up. All I remember is reading my architect drafting book, I must have fallen asleep. Mom looked in my bedroom and saw me fall asleep reading my book, so she didn't bother to wake me up and told Gigi I was asleep. I should have told mom to wake me up. Man! I didn't realize I was that tired yesterday. "Sorry, I snapped at you", my teacher said. "I understand you were on TV yesterday. I did not get the chance to come to the track meet, but I saw it on TV last night. You guys are excellent! I was not able to keep up with it, my kids called me in the living room all excited then I told them you are my student. We sat there and had an excellent time! I think I had more good time than them because I knew some of you. It's a good feeling to see someone you know on TV, that doesn't come around too often! T-Mac, you are faster than the other poor kids, you ran them down real easy!"

I was thinking if she ever stop for some air, I hope so because I can hear myself thinking, "Lady! I have concern about passions, I have no girlfriend! Well, I can have one but not the one I love." Just so there's no misunderstanding, I loved what she was saying. I accidentally found myself on a movie set, just yards away from being a star, but so poor that I cannot even see myself on Compton cable TV because I have no money to pay for cable or gas or lights bills. I'm one of those people who were not very lucky. I will announce everything from rap to sports, live sex shows, well, I'm still a virgin, do not say anything all right, we agreed on that, okay. Well, you know how sex works, you have to learn how to gamble right and must be careful who you fuck. Not like the early days, a mishandled dick will get blowed up just in three days perhaps, full time.

Each has its place, she's a cat who escorts other guys in the alleys. She will eyeball you like a lapdog, to make you an offer but also to see how much money you have. And if she bites you, grab a fistful of hair so you can hold her head steady and continue to move it up slowly allowing that contour to do some flash dancing.

Do you know that I studied playboy before? I founded the 21st century part book! Man! It was a good one, all in my hands, and do you know why I said all that? I realized I have not had sex before. To control the body and thus the mind, I on the other hand, think I have the ability to be international, and I will with the girl that I love, Gigi. I suffer a stinging pain every time I think about her, in the worse degree or manner, physical and spiritual pain. I felt like a coward for not running after Gigi that day she said she doesn't love me anymore. I was too proud to follow her, I was thinking that she was giving me a lesson in humility to be sure I would understand. I wish that I had the circumstances under control, before it become an ultimate misunderstanding between her and Coach. I knew that Gigi is coming back, and she have! But I don't know what's on her mind. Well, English class is over and I took a long, deep breath before stepping out in to a human body of traffic in the hallway that gave me a chance to appreciate the people. A big complex chess game, smiling faces, thugs and players walked through the hallway, not that many geeks though. I promise that if I start being around them, you will be the first to know as well as some of the smartly dressed business people.

Well this is the ghetto, that means that the cops or Bill collect money that you owe. School has a different impression on life as Dad says, "real law-and-order". Welcome to the ghetto, it's all action over the past few years, killing! They also feel proud about how they had accepted full responsibility for their hood. My black people were proud but also bitter, the more victims you have, the bigger your reputation. The project is one big concentration camp, but we are all victims, the cops don't even use the words, "We apologize for killing your child, we thought he had a weapon". That happens more and more when the youngsters don't get it, they join gangs and become more violent.

I look at the traffic of student in this hallway, how many of them killed someone before or perhaps, may be wanted for something else. Fight an idea with a better idea, I'd like to believe that's not true, if it is, "oh well", suddenly I had to piss so I went to the restroom, it doesn't seem like such a good idea to be here, but I had to go real bad. I can smell the marijuana smoke in the air then I heard a loud voice, "What the hell is going on?" I thought. The school cop said, "Yes! I live to drill the bastards who are smoking marijuana in my school campus!" he caught me with my zipper down and my penis in my hand standing over the urinal. I looked behind me wanting to say, "I do not know what the hell are you talking about, I'm no bastard. I have a father and I'm damn sure I do not smoke weed" but I just it to myself. The cops were checking eyes to see if they were high and smelling hands for weed smell on them, so I zip up my pants and told the cop standing behind me, "Like to smell my hands?" As I was pushing them in his face, he stepped back quickly saying "No, no, it's okay, I can see your eyes, you okay T-Mac, I know you are not smoking drugs. By the way, you kicked ass yesterday, keep up the good work son. Do not be like these three thugs, ending up in prison or getting killed" one of them said, "How do you know he is not the one smoking weed?" the cop said. "I know you are not talking about your what not! You tell me how many times I dusted you in here, you are not even smart enough to know better. Take that smile off your face, you look high as hell!" He laughed again, no one could get in or out now. But me, I have a juice card, that cop knew my name, I was beginning to think not all cops are bad.

I had a flashback to being a little boy, I always shit and wet in my pants in first grade, I would cry and not being able to stop, all my classmates called me shitty boy and laughed at me. I had no friends to play with during recess, I sat on the bench the whole time. "Shitty boy dummy!" That was my name. The teacher kept yelling at me when I begin reading "The cat in the hat". Mom always helped me learn how to read, but it didn't help. I'd still get nervous and wet my pants. They put me back on the same grade, "shitty boy dummy", I was believe I was. Mom will be up late helping me for Friday tests just to get big F's on them. All my the teachers told the other kids "He's not a dummy, he's special" so the school district sent a specialist to find out that I have dyslexia. Well, I still have it but I now know how to work with my problems. I still go to my special class on Fridays and my first grade teacher said, "Go play T-Mac, go play now!" I sublimated like crazy as a kid, and then looked for a place to put my anger. I said "Okay", for whatever reason I ran and ran around that playground quickly. I had no friends but I found something I was good at and now love. Running.

"Hey Mr. Finnly, I was thinking can I make a model of my house, I'm drawing for the fair" I said. Mr. Finnly said, "That will be a complex project because the fair is in two weeks on a Friday".

"I can do it", I said.

"Okay T-Mac, go on ahead and make it," Mr. Finnly said, so I stayed there after school. After a moment, I couldn't even hold the pen anymore so I decided to rest, and it occurred to me that my cousin has a drafting table that he is not using. I will ask him to lend me that.

Only a minute or so passed, I went home. I felt the intense urge to call Gigi, what was I expecting to hear, the explosive "No!"? It's six o'clock, Gigi is home at this time, well the last I remember she always is. I made it to the house,

rushed over to pick up the phone and made the call. I felt like I was calling 911, it's nothing life threatening but my heart was pounding. "Hello", Gigi's voice made me smile, "I take it you're not up to this?" I said. "No," she said. You could say I'm a little down on high-tech love activities, but Gigi is another story. I left it there and tried not to make a big deal about it. I didn't want to scare Gigi's heart, it made me want to tear the first player amendment into tiny pieces but I backed off, when I realized that's not what I called her for, I will stay anonymous. Gigi said, "Yes, T-Mac!" "Well, have your mom told you I called yesterday?", "Yes, she have" Gigi said quietly. "Gigi, what I want to say is, would you go to the prom with me?"

Somehow I knew Gigi was used to my influence on her but to hear it out the horse's mouth was different. "It may sound a little strange to you T-Mac, but your new girlfriend would not like you taking your ex-girlfriend to the prom." "Stop it! Stop it! Stop it Gigi!" I just spilled the beans, "Listen here, Gigi! I'm tired of your and coach shit, I am a regular guy or better, I'm still a virgin. My mom does not let me go to parties, and chasing girls! That's bullshit. I'm so in love with you, I had to bug your mom let you call. Coach lied to you and I quit the track team, then they beat me up. My little brother used to look up to me but now he calls me a wussy, because I cry while saying "I love Gigi, I love Gigi". It was a prize fighter but I got it all off my chest weeping, but it was a beautiful thing.

I was at a red light, and it felt good sitting there. My mind was somewhere else, to make a change in my life, and the car behind me was blowing their horn because the light turned green. Well, I slammed the phone down, it may sound a little strange to you, but if you have some suggestions, I'm all ears and I'll bring some of that stuff next time. A long-hair super chicken, didn't seem so bad, "Everybody's got some little things, that really annoys them, like barking dogs, or car alarms, a boss or a neighbor. In the meantime, I called my cousin Curtis and my cousin Ethan picked up the phone, we chatted for a few minutes then I asked him if Curtis was home, Ethan said "Yeah, he's here, you wanna talk to him?" "Let me holla," I said, "What's up! T-Mac", Curtis said. "Nothing much Curtis, I was thinking, do you still use that drafting table you have?" Curtis said, "I put it in the garage, you can have it", I said "That's great!". "So, what's been up with you?" Curtis said, "I'm not trying to cut you off, but I have to go." I said and put the phone down.

On a Saturday morning, I was laying in bed looking up out the window, there are cumulus clouds in the sky. They are thick, white and fluffy, they look like piles of cotton. You can often see cumulus clouds on a sunny summer day, they mean fair weather, and cumulus clouds form much lower in the atmosphere than cirrus clouds and are made only of water droplets when warm air rises and cools. It looks like a good day for running in El Segundo beach.

I'm sitting on the sand, stretching, when I remember a very good friend. You see, it was like this. I was sitting around about here, where I'm sitting now when this guy ran by me. He caught my attention because his running form was perfect. He was looking about ten foot in front of him, and he was moving. I just sat there and finished my stretching. When I look down the beach on the same direction that guy was running, he was pretty far down the beach. I thought, I'm going to tee-off him, catch him and run him down before the three miles mark. The beaches are separated by rocks. At my three miles mark where I was sitting, I ran, stopped and turned around to go back to the starting point. But that day, I lost the race. Sssh, don't tell any one okay! It was a kick ass race. That guy felt me on his ass, I was gaining ground on him. He broke his perfect form. The number one rule is to never look back. He saw me coming up fast so he kicked up a gear too. The rocks were directly in front of us, I was right on his bumper, there was a ten yard distance between us and the rocks. In five yards, we were neck to neck but as a kid I always had day dreams that I can fly. As I was coming to the rocks very fast, I started to slow down but the white guy was still moving fast. I thought he was going to run in to the rocks but he flied right over the rocks. I then knew how the apostles felt when they saw Jesus rays up in the sky. You need to have faith.

That guy turned back running, looking right at me and he made a gun gesture with his hands at me and winked. I stood there looking at him disappeared like a ghost in the light fog. He could not be beaten on this beach, looked like that's what he was saying. I guess he's right. I wish you'd seen his transformation was quite amazing.

I was thinking about the memories, I feasted my eyes on the beauty of the beach. For a little slice of heaven I could see ocean waves hitting the sand. The beach water giving off an eerie light from the sun looked so beautiful. I felt like I was sitting in my dream house into a vast ocean front living room. My thoughts are bigger than life. On the door mat it would say "Turtle Beach House". Oh yeah, I would say it's my choice. You can offer your side of thing and if you don't, that's fine too. I fully recognize these aren't ideal circumstances to determine a man's innocence or guilt for being poor. That was the first intelligent thing I thought about so far, I allow myself to be sidetracked. Once again, I realized this is more than a little unusual. All I can say is I come here to kick these rocks ass three miles down the sand today.

Boom!boom! boom! Boom! George, George, George of the jungle, strong as he can be, watch out for that tree, uh, uh, uh turtle, turtle, turtle of the beach, strong as he can be, watch out for those rocks, uh, uh, uh "Ouch"! I hit a rock on the other side, and broke my leg, "Yikes!", I was trying to control my feelings, I felt as if I was flying over and over them rocks, I beat my feet against the shell-covered sand floor on the other side. Somehow I have to remember to tell myself not to stop fighting the feeling and concentrate, with no reserve, no retreat, no regrets, suddenly the ocean fade away.

I'm on my way home thinking my boss is right. I peeped at them coming in my class, coach and Mr. Finnly are pissed off. Well, let me put you up on game before we get noisy. You see, today is Thursday, I'm in my drafting class getting my project finish for the fair tomorrow, that's not the problem, why they are pissed. The problem is tomorrow is Friday, and that's when we are running at Mountsac College for the 2A C.I.F Championship, to go to state championship, where all level schools are there. That is like the Kids Olympic, but the thing is I cannot be in two places at the same time, the art fair and the track meet, so let us be noisy.

"Come on damn it! Mr. Finnly" coach said.

Then Mr. Finnly responded, "Tmac has his project all ready"

"Why are you saying he has to be there? That makes no sense Mr. Finnly", said coach "Well, Coach Lether, it might not make sense to you, but to me it does because he has to make a presentation at the fair Mr. Lether."

"I see, but can you have someone stand in for one day?"

Mr. Finnly said, "So Mr. Lether, you're saying that it's only one day?"

"Yes, Mr. Finnly", coach said.

You heard yourself, the cleanup operation, it went from red, yellow and black green, that was better than sex, bag it up baby! I looked over coach's old big broad shoulders and read the big, beautiful headline one more time: C.I.F Championship Track Meet, and the stands of people make our stands looked tiny because the college stand is enormously big and the track is rubber. My face twisted, and I thought I was almost going to cry, but a cry of joy. Then I lean over and kiss her for giving a shit, well, I mean for caring. But these stands of people make problems disappear and get coach's attention. I heard coach said, "I know all of you are celebrating, but it's not over until it's over. I know all of you are excited, but keep your concentration on what we come here for today. They are our competition out there, so take a few minutes to get your minds right. There has been a little change in the running order, if I call your name wait right here and give your track shoes to the assistant coach, he will put little spikes in them". And my name was the first name that coach called, "T-Mac!" "Yes, Coach", I said. "Look here son, I know you qualify for six races but today I only want you to run two races."

"The 440 relay and the 1600 hundred relay son, don't ask questions. That's it and that's all." Coach sounded like porky pig, "That's it and that's all folk!" So I gave my shoes to the assistant coach and told him to take good care of Miss Goodwin, that's the name I gave my shoes and I'm afraid I was pissed off thinking why coach suddenly changed his mind on 100 yard, 220, 880, 440 races. I was the number six train, I was just waiting there with my door open hoping that coach changes his mind.

When the doors closed, coach still didn't give in, my equilibrium returned. There's no reason crying over spilled milk, I suppose coach knows what he's doing. What really screwed me up is when coach put one of my teammates that's not even as fast as me in my four other races. This doesn't make any sense, there's no point telling me anything, "that's it and that's all" Coach said. I just need a hug but no one is around to give it to me. I still did as instructed, but my mind was rioting, "Why am I sitting here with my hands on my lap? Why am I cooperating?"

After about ten minutes, I couldn't stay in the hot seat any longer, I walked out. I thought coach was going to yank on the alarm but he knew I was kind of teed off. The assistant coach said, "Hey! Hold up, T-Mac", I couldn't keep back a half smile, "Look at me son!" I decided to sit back down and he said, "The only reason I'm talking to you right now is because of the respect I have for you and the affection I have for your teammates. Son, you're here, this is it! After today, half of these kids season are over! You've come too far to just throw it away son. Coach Lether knows what he's doing okay?" "Yeah, all right", I said. "T-Mac, don't be so naïve as to believe that you cannot be beaten son, and this is a friendly warning. Life has its consequences, I promise you." Well, I said to myself, I guess we've both been worried that I lose a race. "I'm glad we had this little chat coach", I said.

I wish I could tell him that when I pushed my way through the finish line to get my first plays metal but the revolving door went like this in the 440 relay. I came out the starting block, for the first 100 yard. Yes! You know I kick ass, and all the other three of my teammates ran good, the anchor man brain it in for the win. Yes! we won but it's nothing like going through the finish line with the ribbon across your chest, you just can't die out, you have to go an extra yard immediately, it's a big relief to see your teammate make it home. A joy for one is a joy for all. All the fire comes out of you, only a member knows that the biggest exciting race of the day is that everybody is waiting on, and it's the last race of the day. 1600 hundred relay and coach has me running second. The officials keep calling for all schools to put their running order list in, it got to a point when the officials said that our school will be disqualified if he does not put in the running order, so coach sent the assistant coach to see how many schools run there. When he comes back, he and coach were laughing for the first time out of three years. I heard coach said something good about me, about being fast, I mean they were talking to each other and not to me. It's about the other schools wanting to match their fastest guys up against me, coach was playing a little cat and mouse game, the officials call for all head coach to come to the officials stand.

The Official said, "Now look here, we have been asking all of you to turn in the 1600 hundred relay running order. You turn it in now or get disqualified right now!" When coach came back he had a big smile on his face, which is odd because he always had a serious look on his face when he was up there with the officials. His hands were like dancing and he seemed to be waiting for the last minute before he gives up any information. I can see all the other coaches peeking when coach put the page down so calmly and walked off with a smile. He needs to smile more often I think, he looks cool.

The assistant coach had us warmed up while people were taking snapshots. I felt 135 pounds horsepower in my legs, I was ready to do the competition. "Eat my dust!" everything unfolds in perfect sequence to hear "9", that means to take off running because my teammate came up on me fast, when he said "10", I threw my hand back for the baton to be passed, so smooth, so fresh and so clean. I'm out of here! Well you know how it is, we are going to the "State"!

When I got up this morning, my little brother was looking at the TV for his favorite cartoon show and didn't want to play with me as long as his show is on. "What's up little bro?" Anthony said, "They kicked your butt yesterday?" "You know Lil' Bro, I made them, eat my dust!" I replied. I was looking forward for a funny remark from him but he said, "They are letting you win, just like when you let me beat you up. Remember when I kicked you In your balls." I said, "We are two young players laughing and joking all the way, you tried to kick them only once and I didn't mind that because you did not hurt my balls so badly. But I don't mind telling you that I really want to kick your ass!" I smiled, the mood in the room was thoughtful and it was lovely that we had gained a much richer feel, where all the pieces fit in this big jigsaw puzzle of love and war.

"Yeah, mama!" "Come here boy!" I freely admit that every time I had to go to mom's room, the thought of "Not me" pops up in my head. The closer I get, the more it felt like it was exactly 1.4 nautical miles, or twenty-eight hundred yards. "Yes, mom!", I said. "Boy, this girl named Gigi keeps calling, is this the girl that you were bugging me to call? She never called but now she keeps calling back to back yesterday. I told her you were at a track meet at some college. I told her I do not have any girls in this house, what is she calling here for because you know that Jehovah does not like any girl and boy stuff or have you had sex boy?" mom said. "Of course not, mom!" I exclaimed. "Well, she said that too when I asked her. Well boy, she said it was something to do about a prom" mom said. The way I see it, mom told her exactly what I said so now she will believe me, I made up my mind that I am not going to the prom without Gigi.

"Hello, Gigi! I believe we have to talk about some real business." "Okay", Gigi said "but I felt better about us after I talked to your mom yesterday, I think your mom is a pretty good person."

"Yeah, I agree", I said. "T-Mac, I miss you so much! Do you still love me, like you said that day at your track meet in front of all the people T-Mac?" she said. "Yes, Gigi! I always loved you and I never stop loving you, not once. You are so pretty baby, far more than anything to me, Gigi" I replied. Tears were still running down my cheeks, "I'm sorry, T-Mac. What do I have to do to prove it to you? I still love you too!"

"That reminds me Gigi, go to the prom with me okay?"

"Yes, T-Mac, I would love to!" she wasn't sniffling anymore. "Gigi, you are always around when I needed you on my track meets, you help me to win, it will be completely insane not to take you to my prom. I confess, I extremely love you Gigi and I have to admit, you look as good as ever, Gigi."

"Thank you, T-Mac! I will wear something with my favorite color, red hot pink! You like that color on me, right? I think it makes me look pretty!" I said, "I love that color on you Gigi, do you have a dress like that which you can wear to the prom?" "No T-Mac, I was going to ask you what we are going to wear. My mom said it's not her prom and she is not buying me anything."

I must have given her the wrong impression because here she is showing her support for me and the only thing I can think of is that I will buy the prom dress for her. "Gigi," I said, "I will get it for you okay?" She was all excited, I felt great too! But where the hell am I going to get the money for that dress? Oh Jesus I was thinking this just keeps getting worse. I whispered back to Gigi, "Do you remember our first kiss?" I've been wanting to do it for a long time. I kissed Gigi gently on the lips, her lips were soft and fit perfectly with mine, and we stayed that way for a sweet moment before we pulled back and looked at each other. Gigi whispered back and said, "The night of the prom my King", I was all smiles, she called me her king! All this time I would have thought she will say "Hero", at that moment I was beginning to know Gigi all over in a romantic way, I want to be with her for a long time!

"Congratulations, asshole", I said to myself, "Am I getting warm? It's getting hot in here! I told you I can be international if I wanted it so badly, with Gigi all over her world. I was afraid to even hope for it but I asked her anyway, "Gigi are you still my girlfriend?" "Yes, I am T-Mac!" Gigi said.

I felt like the Madonna song "Like a virgin! Touched for the very first time!". I know we would be good together but I had no idea how good it could be for the first time in my life, I was in love. We bid our goodbyes then I told her I'd call her tonight. It was her gentleness that touched me deeply. The following minutes, I was calling my Boss. I was thinking, all my life mom was buying me second hand clothes. This morning,

nothing I had on costs more than six dollars so I decided to ask my Boss to help me get Gigi a dress.

"What's up Mr. Gregory?".

"I'm doing okay" he said.

"I call to see if you have some work for me? I need some money for my prom. It's coming soon".

"I'm happy you called just in time T-Mac! I do have this job and I sure need your help."

"Okay, I'm your man!" I said.

"Hey T-Mac, I saw your name in the newspaper today, you guys are going to the state championship, boy that's a dream come true! Do you remember the talk we had the last time T Mac?" He said.

"Yes sir, but it's going to be weeks before our state meet, Mr. Gregory!" I replied.

"Okay T-Mac, you help me with this job and I'll make that prom night a romantic one for you and your girlfriend Gigi. How is she doing?"

"Oh, she's okay", I said. "You see her mother said that it is not her prom so she is not going to buy Gigi a dress, that's why I need money Mr. Gregory."

"Well, there's more to that T-Mac, you need more things too son, like how are you getting to the prom?"

"Well, I do not know, I have not thought about that one," we laughed.

"Look T-Mac," Mr. Gregory said, "you help me okay and I will look out foreverything." "Everything you said?!"

"Yes T-Mac, everything, photographs and all!" "Thank you Mr. Gregory!"

"Hey son, you do not have to thank me because you are not asking something for free, and even if you did I would still do it for you. I have a cousin who makes dresses, a tailored made dress. So call Gigi and tell her, she has to go get sized up today."

My heart was pumping fast, "Okay," I said, "I'll call you right back after I call Gigi". "All right, T-Mac!" Mr. Gregory replied.

I was nervously looking at Gigi because I felt it. I guess she kissed me softly on my cheek and took a seat beside me, we leaned against one another more than we ever had. I couldn't begin to imagine being separated from her anymore. I took her hand and squeezed it to show my compassion. I watched Gigi's pretty eyes concentrating on the road and her hair whipping around in the breeze, and I realized the only honest thing for me to do was to shut up, be happy and smile, we finally made it to the fabric store. Gigi jumped out of the truck and asked if I was coming inside, "If you give me a reason to go inside" I said, she laughed and said "If you help me pick out my fabric and color, I will have a surprise for you after the prom." I was out of that truck even before Gigi could turn around. We picked this hot pink silk fabric that looked so beautiful against her skin, I loved it. Mr. Gregory and I dropped her off at the house of Gregory's cousin for her to get sized up for her dress and she will get to see her dress get made, at least some of it, for six hours or so. I told Gigi that but she said that she understands. The love of my life gave me a half-smile and I returned it. I felt as if she was back for good trying to walk this tight rope six hours between us, but I had to go to work. No discussion about that, we both know. I told her I love her, I thought too much was left unsaid, we had to make up for all the lost time between us, but she knew that I work for Mr. Gregory. I guess you can call a so-called establishment, Mr. Gregory works for himself, a general contractor of black entrepreneurs. I looked at him and he looked back at me while I'm saying my good bye to Gigi. I knew it only be a few hours, so what? I just love my Girl so much. Mr. Gregory was sitting in his truck listening to his favorite music, dancing up and down in the truck singing, "If you hear in need noise it's just me and the boys! Hit me, hit me!" Mr. Gregory likes that song because I remember one summer we were working on a house in an upper class neighborhood, "Six in the morning the police was at my door, my fresh Adidas went across the bathroom floor, well that's Ice-T's story."

But my story is this, we were remodeling a bathroom for a customer who was at work in about six in the morning. We were using high power tools when one of the neighbors called the police. They came and were banging on the door for a long time but we could not hear them knocking until we stopped cutting on the wall. Bang, bang, bang! "What the hell is that?" I said. Mr. Gregory went to the front door to the police, as soon as the police men left, Mr. Gregory went outside to his truck blasting his music. "If you hear any noise, it's just me and the boys" he said. Mr. Gregory was a lawyer that day, he told those policemen a thing of two about the law. We can work with high power tools from 6:00 AM until 11:00PM. It would be funny to see him in the street saying "Hit me, hit me!" and Blacky will get too excited and start barking. Blacky is our dog, he jumped on the back of the truck one day while we were on a job, and he had been one of the boys since them. Blacky's job is looking out for the tools on the back of the truck, and he does it really well. I love Blacky.

Unfortunately, when we picked up Gigi, she told me she has a new boyfriend and asked if I'd like to see him. My mind was running a hundred miles an hour but my Boss' cousin and Gigi, they were all smiling I guess about the look that is dancing across my face, Gigi calls him "sweet heart," The bedroom door open. He come out sipping Coca-Cola and grinning at me, I walked towards Gigi and hug her and kiss her, suck his tongue out at me, everybody began laughing again, I get up of my chair, ran over there, and said, "Come here you little player!", and balled my fist up, lil' man kicks rock, ran to his room, and I told Gigi, "You see, he's a chicken." He heard me call him chicken so he opened the door and said, "You chicken punk!"

Everyone was laughing and applauding, only in the ghetto. He is a handsome little boy, around about five-years-old, well it was a hard days work. We took Gigi back home to long beach, when we get to the projects there were police cars in front of our building and I saw my neighbor at the back of the police car, and his fat ass wife at the top of the steps talking shit with a black eye saying, "That's why I'm fucking him, you're a little dick ass or you're gay because you're not fucking me, you tired all the time! You're fucking someone."

Now, that bitch is a lying crazy ass, that man is working two jobs for that fat bitch can ride around in a new car, with that nigga she's fucking and when that ghetto hoe asks her if she's fucking her man, that bitch acted like she was all uncomprehending to shit. Well, I'm telling you, it was going to be on, man. I hate to say that I miss that ass kicking, that bitch has three kids but not one is his. Gheto bitches have a good man but do not know how to keep them, man. I'm happy Gigi is not like that, it's not over till it's over. Watch and see when that ghetto hoe, get an ear about that shit, it's on!

That's another story," Afterward I watched television for a while then lay on the bed thinking about Gigi, with the Los Angeles Times folded open to the sport, looking for our Track meet, there we were after that to the crossword puzzle, and the end of a pencil between my teeth about midnight I turned out the light and said my prayers. "Amen, God is good all the time!"

If you're not satisfied by this time, I'm going to throw this at you. I had spent two hours at the hairdresser for my hair. It is now two inches and looking good, not just a cut but a hairdo because today is the big day. Today is my prom night, that's right, my prom night. Have you not observed any difference in my appearance? Look at the walk player! I'm so cool. Am I annoying you hoes? Well, I better get away from this mirror before I will be late in picking Gigi up, I figured that it doesn't sound good at all. My Mac line in the mirror, I mean from the look on your faces it's got to be serious, and I don't want you to think that I'm concerned, it's just that I'm starving like Alfalfa and Darla on the little rascals. I'm in love. I saw my little brother and his prom date sitting in the 8b Lincoln continental, my best friend asked my little brother to be her date for the pro. I love to have him there, well, she lives in the projects too.

I decided to rent a car Lincoln, not a Limo because we will have the Lincoln for the weekend after party. We can go where ever we want to go without a Limo driver on the clock. We picked up Gigi, She looks like a princess, so precious and elegant, yet so beautiful in that dress. It is so pretty, the red hot pink dress is as silky as Gigi's smooth skin. Her silky hair is down her back, she looked like she came from paradise. Her nails are pink with red tip and she's wearing pink sandals with her favorite cartoon character Tweety bird holding a rose. "I thought I thaw a puddy tat!" Her toe nails are the same as her hands, her feet were pretty not because they were newly polished but because I have not seen her feet before. They were beautiful, she always has shoes on. I remember her telling me that she has a surprise for me on the day of the prom. I hope it's something manly, not girly.

I told her "You look so beautiful Gigi," "Thank you, T-Mac", Gigi said, "you are so handsome my king", I smile and kiss her right in the mouth, her lips were made for me, soft and fit perfectly with mine. The only thing missing was her tongue bathing in my mouth, but the night is still young, like I said, it's not over till it's over. Gigi had only little make up which she did not really need anymore, she has a beauty of her own, I love her and I have something special for her when we get to the Queen Mary in Long beach. You're right if you guessed that our prom is on the Queen Mary, I have never been to the Queen Mary but I was told that she's a beautiful ship. I pinned a rose on my angel Gigi and she pinned a pink one on me.

Off to Queen Mary we went. I died and got resurrected in heaven, everybody was looking at us as we come in the door way flashing their cameras. All of my schoolmates in the class of 8b were telling stories of their new lives out of school and on to a new world for us. You know me, when the camera is on me, I am all smiles with an angel in my arm. Her perfume smells so sweet to my nose that it makes me want to eat her up. It makes my heart fuzzy when her pretty face is looking at me and she's holding my arm in a romantic night. An assigned table had My name on top so we sat down, I told Gigi I'll be back then I went to the car to get my friends ghetto box for my surprise for Gigi.

On the Queen Mary, I went to the top front deck, put the music box down and went back inside. I took Gigi by her hand and walked her back outside. We looked at the beautiful stars in the sky with my arm around her. I gave her a kiss, I have been waiting for her to lay her hand on me too, my penis went hard quickly. I was powerless under the power she had over me, I was afraid to move, I knew she felt my penis hard against her body, it had a mind of its own and wriggled hard, if it wriggles harder she will be swept overboard. I told her "You are so beautiful tonight, huh?" Gigi said, "Mmhh", in a very sexy way. I guess Gigi feels hotter than me now, I told her I like to get her surprise right here and now. I turn on the music box I made this for us, and ask her, "Would you like to dance with me under the stars my love?", and I took her hands and push play on the music box, "Lady in red is dancing with me... cheeks to cheeks nobody here but you and me dancing cheeks to cheeks….." To feel Gigi's soft face on mine is making it a joyful beginning of romantic love I never experienced before, like a bride and groom. Like each one keeps seeking not for his own advantage, but that of the other person, that was what I owe Gigi for all the time she has been there for me. Even if I could afford more to be real, I would not change anything that night. Hell no! I will eliminate that feeling for nothing on earth. I greatly appreciate Gigi's love with no regrets at all, it's a mixture of joy, I recall there were tears but in addition of those of sadness in Gigi's eyes, I kiss them away from her face, I wish them to be tears of joy.

With the love in my eyes, the joy was so great, it seems like a dream come true, the best day of my life! Gigi and I up on the beach after the prom was over. Two bodies lay in the sand, feeling so hot with passion, with our clothes on the sand, she lays on top of me. Her body is so sexy and smooth, she smells so fresh, her breasts in my mouth, my hands on her smooth tight butt, I squeezed it firmly as she opens up her legs.

With my penis in her hand she moves slowly and she continues to put it inside her slowly, it feels so hot and wet. It is tight, she moves up and down slowly on top of my penis. "Oh,Oh,Oh" Gigi asked "Is it good T-Mac?" "Oh yes Gigi!" She cut me off, and said, "It's your daddy!" My teeth and body started to shatter, I could not believe what is happening to me, with a maximum satisfaction. I was coming like crazy, "Oh,oh,oh Gigi!" Like a virgin, making love for the very first time, like a viiiirgin! Well, it's been one week of party after party and Gigi riding the shit out of me, playing our favorite song "Babyface". "It's better than love, sweet as can be, You've got that whip appeal, so whip it on me!"

The state track meet is in two days, and I haven't been to any practice. I'm feeling drained, no energy, and my legs feel weak. I need to go running today from Newgema Village, the name of the project I live in. I will run to Harthorne Mall, I will run down El'Segundo Street to Harthorne Street, the mall is the one in the corner. Up and back will be five miles from the projects, well, I will run two miles up El'segundo. I was in parking lot of the mall, I bent over out of breath with no energy and my legs felt weak. All I could think about is Gigi and I, we have to stop our love making.

Man, as much as I enjoy her, I have to make a sacrifice for the team. I know Gigi will understand me, I always had this run up and back with no problem but today was different, my legs started to cramp up with a vague gnawing in my stomach, only one part of my mind was permitted to dwell on these horrors. What have I done? It never occurred to me that nowhere in all these thoughts, was concern for my own safety. The girl I love is draining me out my strength, although I have made a consideration for the team and for myself. I smiled for the first time, it's going to be okay, in two days I will be get my strength back. I will tell Gigi that we need to stop having sex, it will really stir up the shit if I lose in the state meet, it's my responsibility to tell Gigi, I didn't want to look like a fool in Gigi eyes.

After stretching in the mall parking lot, I ran back home to the project for the other two and a half miles, well I think I'm beginning to feel a little better but I still know for a fact that sex is draining me, not improving me. I'm almost home, I started doing my cool down, my body is more relax this time. Hell those cramps are some new shit to me. I'm lying in the tub with hot water and one cup of bleach like coach said to take out cramps in your muscles. I have one more day to gain my legs muscles strength back, this physical fitness is crazy! Like coach said, missing one day is like missing one week and on top of the sex, sex, sex, I was thinking with a big smile on my face. Oh, do not tell my mom I'm fucking boy, "The phone is for you, T-Mac" mom said, "Okay, mom! Hello" "You got that whip appeal so work it on me", I can hear Gigi singing Baby face song on the phone to me, I try to cut her off but she was too emotionally involved in the song, "Gigi! Gigi!" I said, "Yes T-Mac!" she said, "I have something to tell you Gigi, can we slow down having sex just for two days? Tomorrow I have to go to my state track meet and yesterday while I was running, I felt so drained and I have no strength in my legs Baby. You have been wearing me out Gigi." "Okay, what do you mean?" Gigi said, "Baby, just for a few days that's all I said", just as Gigi began to speak in a voice a little louder than normal, I realized that it is happening like one of those silences when a conversation reach a pause simultaneously, so that her volume made her seem to be making an announcement instead of simple statement. "Oh you get my shit and now you are saying that you are cool on my loving. I know I'm sexy! You guys get at me all the time, I need some loving T-Mac, right now! I know you can't say no to me!" "Yes, Gigi!" I said, "but only for

37

two days! That's all baby, do you not want to see me be a state champion and go to the top ten colleges. I want to go to." She exclaimed, "I don't give a damn! It's always about you T-Mac, well fuck you! I hope you lose tomorrow! They already paid me to wear your ass out! I fuck the shit out of your ass and keep you partying! That's why I came back!" then Gigi hang up in my face. Damn it! Why did she say all that to me? I expect she'll be calling me back today to apologize but that's neither here nor there, Gigi is mad at me. I thought she would understand but I lost track of what I was saying to myself, I started putting together some double take in disbelief. "Man, I don't get no credit from Gigi" I keep on saying to myself "Let her call me back, but I had to call her back. "Gigi" I said, then she will say, "So are you coming over, T-Mac?", "No, Gigi" I said, then she will say "What the fuck do you want?". Gigi is a thug or a rent-a-thug wannabe. This time, I didn't bother to talk so she hang up. She feels as hot as the sun, she was as mad as I was hurt, she was not the loving person I once knew. I don't know what else to do, Gigi was the one that always pushes me to win, now she wishes for me to lose. Why am I'm feeling that there's something more to this than sex? "They already paid me", what did she mean about that? I will worry about that later, Gigi and her worries about not having sex, if she is really my girl, she will be here, especially since we didn't make any love today in the first place. I told myself over and over to let go, the more I said that the more I found myself thinking about Gigi. "Why Gigi, why Gigi! When I need you by my side right now? To see your beautiful smile, your pretty face keeps popping in my mind, my princess, my precious and elegant yet so beautiful, I'm going fuckin' crazy!" My heart is saying, "Call her back and make love to her passionately, you know you want to call her, rip her clothes off make love and make here submit to me, saying "it's your Daddy" as I ride the shit out of her. Call her back T-Mac! Call her back!" It keeps running over and over in my head, I was sad and too tired to smile. I am hurt emotionally, abused by Gigi this time, she lowered my self-esteem, bruised heart and I am afraid Gigi does not love anymore like she said. She is a stranger, that was not my Gigi, I'm only dreaming. "Wake your ass up, wake up T-Mac, right now!" But apparently not, Gigi and I are having a sex argument, who is the victim? Me or her? I can try to protect myself against violent crimes, but what crime have I done again for her to act like that? There's something more to this, I'm going to get to the bottom of this, "They paid me!", keeps popping up in my head. What she means about that shit was probably just nothing. I lay in bed all day, no strength, energy or wellness. I feel uncomfortable so I try to force myself to eat, I didn't care that I was sick, very sick, beaten down by Gigi, pushed to give up on my dreams. I have a burning heart and I am very sad that a doctor cannot heal me, but only Gigi can. Ring you damn phone, just ring! Be my love on the line! I called her over a hundred times but she hanged up in my face.

Mr. Telephone man, there's something wrong with my line because when I call mu baby's number I get a click every time.

Unfortunately, I had a dream, some other god forsaken place, I sat up in bed and was trying to justify why the endless run, I was running backwards! The finish line was getting farther and Gigi was behind calling me. I trying to go to the finish line but its seems like Gigi is putting me back like a Voodo T-Mac. I sit up in bed, weak because of lack of sleep, I try real hard to go back to sleep. "Win, I'm going to win!" I repeat to myself with absolutely no emotion in my thoughts. Oh, fuck! The alarm clock goes off, I hit the top to shut it and look up out the window. The sun is starting to come out, I was looking out with one eye, still feeling sleepy. I lay there for a few minutes then I realized that Gigi is in trouble for getting me really bombed out, as I called it and don't want to look foolish in my track team's eyes, coach was right!

The school looks like a ghost town because there's no one in the hallways. I make it to the gym and knock on coach's office. Coach opens the door, I try to come in his office but he pushes me back in my chest. I was slightly out of focus and felt pain in my chest. I was confused why coach hit me in my chest, his eyes are like fire! I looked at him with mouth wide open, we looked at each other as I am equally stunned. Had someone seen me and Gigi fucked on the sand at the night on the prom? Maybe they were on the beach too then told Coach and they stepped away so I will not see them. But at that moment of passion we had, I think I won't give a damn whoever sees us. I was beginning to feel that Coach is going to put his hands on me so I asked him quietly, "What's up, Coach?" I looked into his flashing eyes, I saw the invitation there like he was saying, I will kick your ass boy. Coach extended his hand and poked at my chest very hard, I had an embarrassed look across my face, I will remember for a long time what Coach said next, I looked foolish, I was blinded by Coach all this time. For three years of my life I believed in this man for it to just end like this. God forgive me but this is something you can't understand, how I can just kill a man! Coach said, "I used your little ass to get to the state meet, you can get the fuck out of here! Your ass is not going to Washington D.C. Take your ass back to the project, you are not on this track team anymore! Be happy I got you in a college, it might not be a Top Ten college, but it's a college! Got your ass out of the ghetto. I had to pull some strings boy! Be happy for that and get the fuck out my office!"

With an empty mind, I was walking with nowhere to go,

I didn't want to go home just to lay in bed and cry so I end up at the park that surrounds the project and sit by the big lake, I sit here until the sun was over my head. I was so hurt that no more tears fall from my eyes, I was having flashbacks about coach and Gigi and all. On the night if the prom, Gigi cried when we were on the Queen Mary's Top front deck when I played that romantic song "Lady in Red is dancing with me". She has started to fall in love over again but she came back to me because she made a promise to someone that she cannot break, I can see sadness in her eyes so I kissed them. That's why I don't understand when she said that they paid her to make me lose, and Coach said that there has been some change in the running order. He said, "if I call your name, wait right here", and my name was the first name that Coach called. He took me out of all my individual races and kept me in the relays only because he can substitute a runner on the relay, that's why he took me out of my other races, he planned it from the start! Has the same person paid him too? I was at a red light while the police is behind me with two dead bodies in my car trunk. When life seems good it's gone all bad at a red light.

"T-Mac", my little brother said, "Michelle is here for you". "What's up Turtle? I heard what coach and that bitch Gigi did, that's fucked up! Why does your ass haven't been coming to school? But you know what, I'm going to put you back up on the game. Oh! those bitches are going to lose in the state meet ha,ha,ha, fuck them Turtle! They know they need your ass, well I have some good news my nigga, you have a scholarship, I mean scholarship Turtle! The principal said that he is not going to call them all, why are you not smiling nigga? Fuck Coach and Gigi! "They cannot stop your ass! You are the man! I can see you are not in a good mood, I love you Turtle, give me a hug, mmmh,"

I can see clearly now that the rain is gone, I can see all the obstacles in my way, it's going to be a bright sunny day in Camp Bloomfield, Malibu, California, foundation of the junior minds. Well, you might be thinking why the hell I am up at the camp and not at college. I hope I'm not a big disappointment to you, I left my Goodwin at El Segundo Beach, so if you find one on the sand, those track shoes were owned by one of the fastest boy in the world. I decided to retire and get away from it all, I'm sitting on top of a water tower looking out at the beach, if you could see me kick up sand or running you down from a distance, that would be because you are my target. Camp Bloomfield is so beautiful up here, with fresh air and bright stars at night, people ride horses and fish in a pond, it is like heaven in this camp. I am still hurting inside, no one knows about the pain I had burning in my heart. Michael Jackson has dropped out of Jehova's Witnesses. A representative of the Woodland Hills congregation where Michael Jackson belonged said that Michael Jackson 'disassociated' himself from the congregation and "no longer considers Michael Jackson to be one of Jehovah's Witnesses." The letter was obtained by the Times. I was thinking to myself, "this is worse than being disfellowshipped or kicked out, man!" "Michael", I said to myself. "It's not going to be Michael or myself at the Dodger Stadium." However, Michael Jackson was quoted in the May 22nd 1984 issue of AWAKE!!! Awake was a Witness magazine, saying that Jackson would never make such a record and video again, like the winning album 'Thriller'. The video depicted Michael Jackson being transformed into a wolf--monster. Michael said, "He want to do what is right in God's eyes", like myself right now thinking about all the good times I had. All the good times I had with Michael Jackson at the assembly with my brother Anthony and my cousin Ethan. We used to serve him sandwiches at the assembly at Dodgers stadium and Michael Jackson said 'fellas, make sure you bring me the grape, the green grapes without no seeds. The ones' without no seeds fellas". He always wanted to hang with us to go from lunch--stands and serve the sandwiches at the assembly for lunch time that had lunch break at the assemblies. It was always a lot of Jehova's Witness kids that always kept coming to The Siege where Michael Jackson and his family was sitting enjoying the assembly that used to always have to interrupt the assembly and tell the parents of the kids to make sure they let their kids stay in the seats and not disturb the Jackson family because they want to enjoy the assembly. But, all the time we used to have to go the van that Michael had. He used to sit in the van and every time he was so happy to see us come in and give him his lunch. We always had a good time talking and laughing. I had those good old days and then one day we went to the van and he wasn't there. All of three of us, Anthony, Ethan and myself, in trying to give him his lunch we said, "is that Michael Jackson standing over on the wall?", and that was the last time I seen him. When he made the Thriller and then he got dis--fellowship and for myself I had to make a decision to run in the 84 Olympic team that the Elders of the Jehovah Witness said and told me that I would have to carry the flag. Ask me you know being a witness we couldn't celebrate the flag or said and told me that I would have to carry the flag and ask me you know being a witness we couldn't celebrate the flag or salute the flag. They decide to step out the room and they told me if I run in the 84 Olympics, I would have to carry the flag. What is I'm going to do is make up my decision going to choose God first or you going to carry the flag so I had to make a decision not to run in the 84 Olympic team although the 84 Olympic team came up to my high school Centennial in Compton and I ran down everybody on the track field and everybody that was from the Olympics track star like Carl Lewis and all the other track stars that was there at the assembly at my high school. I ran them down, made them eat my dust. One guy from Cambodia bet me my Apple (the fruit) he will beat me for my Apple in a 440 race for his Olympic medal and you know what? I ate my Apple, but I'll let him keep his Olympic shirt. Where he come from they couldn't afford medals and they country is poor so their track T--shirts was their Olympic medal. I won the race. I let him keep his medal track field in the 84.

It was my playground, man. I'm going to miss Michael Jackson and thinking about this and we both went through all this as a Witness. We knew each other as a Witness and now here I am retiring my track shoes from the game and Michael and I are making the decision. I know why Michael Jackson made his decision. That is because he knew he had the love for God. I'm making the decision like my friend Michael Jackson, too. I have to laugh at my experience of me and Michael Jackson and now I had to make a decision like having sex and thinking about it was all fun and good now. I see why Michael Jackson made his decision and just like I did for the love of God, Jehovah; memories of Michael Jackson song 'You Got To Enjoy Yourself' in God's house, Enjoy Yourself with me and MJ going around acting a fool in God's house. No college coach who talks all about the mumbo jumbo shit and politics in the sports world, here I am, nobody but T-Mac.

I volunteer for the summer as a counselor, I work with special kids, some deaf, some blind and some are both deaf and blind but they are some of the happiest kids I've seen in my life. When life seems to be at a red light or a stop sign, it seems not to turn green again, it's flashing right in your face. I felt a little better about myself and life, why can't I be happy too? These kids have bigger problems than me but still happy, well I will pick up my game. These kids love me, not because I'm some track star but because I'm a caring person who loves to help, and it was not about who win or lose but about togetherness with these kids, and that's what I love most. Well, sometimes when the cute little kids were all asleep, I would go to the water tower to see the moonlight shine on the ocean thinking about my life, the loneliness I feel inside.

For once in my life I miss the projects and my family. It feels like heaven here in Malibu Beach, the richest beach in beautiful California. Remember the Elephant man? This is the camp where they filmed the movie, right now I'm on the bridge where he ran across to, I remember him and that movie. Well, he is still a legend here, a hero. I walk to the horse stable, there she is a quarter breed horse named Pumpkin, watching that horse puts a big smile on my face. I remember the crush I had on fifth grade teacher at swimming class, her name was Pumpkin. I was her "little bad ass", that's what she calls me, I always moon her going home. The next day, she made me stand in the corner with a cone hat on my head that said dumb. I hope she was okay, I was thinking, I made her do first aid on me, I acted like I was drowning so she jumped in and saved me, I acted like I stopped breathing so she pushed my head back, closed my nose with her fingers, covered my mouth with her mouth and breathed the kiss of my life. I just laid there for one more mouth to mouth but Anthony and Ethan were getting scared so I opened my eyes to look at them and winked my eye but Miss Pumpkin saw me. You know what happened next, I was in the corner for a week for that one, but if you think about it, it was worth it. I never missed a day knowing that my little ass was going to stand in that corner with a dumb cone on my head. I loved Miss Pumpkin, I ended up winning her heart, "her little boyfriend" that's what they called me, but still her "little bad ass," I was standing here smiling about the thoughts I have in mind as I was looking at the horse, Pumpkin.

"She is a beauty", a voice behind me said, I turned around and saw a girl, she is beautiful! You never see women like her in the projects. She has blue eyes, long blonde hair, a sexy body, beautiful breasts, about 5'9, 130 lbs. and her skin is a smooth ivory tan. Her voice is a voice of its own but beautiful in its own way. "Hi, my name is Mary", she said, "She is a beauty huh? Pumpkin has been up here for two years but I still do not let the kids ride her, she used to be a racing horse and she's retired but she is still fast that's why only I can ride her. Oh, by the way, what's your name? As you can see I like to talk, I work out here with the horses all by myself, if I have not introduced myself yet, it's Mary, what's your name?" "Nice to meet you Mary," I said, "T-Mac is my name". "Well T-Mac, it's obvious that you work here, right?" "Yes Mary, I do", she smiled so I smiled back.

She is not as what you see on television, a blonde head dummy. She seems witty. "Well T-Mac", she said, "would you like to meet Pumpkin?" "Yes, Miss Mary". "T-Mac, that makes me sound old, please call me Mary", we smiled then she showed me how to give Pumpkin an apple out of my hand, I should be flat handed so she cannot bite me. Mary and I were becoming best friends, I spend all my extra time helping Mary with the horses. I learn a little about horses and her, I guess you can say, I was falling in love with Mary not knowing her feelings for me. I help her move the hay stack and feed the horses in the morning. Mary always have jeans on, she bends over to move a pitch fork and her eyes caught me staring at her butt. I was thinking if she is into kinky sex like I see in sex video, yeah, her neck, right, squeeze her neck! Yeah! And sometimes a plastic bag, you know, or a pillow, put it over her head and clamp it, hold it around her neck while you spank her ass and fuck her until she call you "Daddy", until she turns red in the face, claws at her back and both of you gasp and wheeze. I don't care about all that myself, but I'm telling you, this girl has a pussy from behind. I mean she can get me off for a wild ride, but for me, too much is always on the edge. Maybe this time, Mary is going to know

I am interested in her, she said, "I see you are looking at my ass", I said, "Huh?" Mary said, "You know what I'm saying T-Mac", I smiled, my eyes flicked off Mary's butt, I realized that Mary is giving me the creeps. I tried to make sense what she was saying, but her words were tumbling out and I couldn't keep up. She kept talking fast, "T-Mac", Mary said, "you like my butt man because you are staring at it" "Yes, I mean no," "Yeah, I saw you T-Mac", I stepped back trying to reconsider my yes and no answer. Mary said, "Look me in my eyes and tell me, you didn't like what you see." I was looking at Mary in the eyes, she's so pretty, no makeup on, but her perfume smells so beautiful. I can just hold her in my arms and lick her all over her neck, passionately kissing her sexy pink lips and still be looking at her pretty blue eyes, like I am now. "Yes, Mary, I loved what I saw, you have a sexy body Mary", I had eyes of passion, her eyes were like she was reading my thoughts and they were undressing me. I can feel the heated passion in her eyes as she felt in mine, we break eye contact when we heard voices of kids coming to ride the horses.

Her face has high cheekbones, she has narrow hips and her butt looks so right in those jeans. She was wearing a man's cowboy shirt, she looked back once then walked quickly with her head down to the other side, through a line of horses, saying "Come on, come on, you're okay," to a half dozen of kids who are very happy that they are going to ride a horse. Their little faces always put a smile on my face. On the other hand, for Mary and me, the question is never finished. This summer is hot, I looked for a tree to go sit under, to get out of the sun and I saw everybody standing around the tree. Then I notice that there is a cabin and some benches that are not in the sun, but it is in a corner. It's all right, it is a beautiful day, I am sitting here thinking about the best of a good life, well, not like the life that I see in the ghetto ramshackle apartments, with fresh air, old clapboard houses outdoor overlooking the river and the hillside. It looks like a big beautiful island with the women and children playing. The kids were an early to bed, early to rise type of kids, and we had to get up too. We had some different ideas about welfare, anyway the families of those kids have money, oceans of money, and it is a far better life than I ever had. I was having a good time with all the kids who were not riding the horses when I heard footsteps from a horse crunched towards us, it was Mary, she said, "They've been with you all day, T-Mac," "Yes, I love my little people, they are telling me about their family and where they live," Mary smiled and said, "You sure made yourself comfortable in my cabin" "Oh yeah, Mary your door was open so we got out of that sun, I hope you don't mind, we also cleanup the things that were on the floor." "Thank you", Mary said with an affirmative smile and told us to come back soon. I said, "I experience some psychological operations in this horse cabin." I said in a playful voice. We all laughed, there is always one coward in every crowd of kids or thugs, but not here, we are all loved and we have each other's back. I told them that's what "homies" are for, I told them in ghetto English and American English class and they love it. I became the coolest counselor at Camp Bloomfield, all the kids keep coming to me and when they have another counselor, they would say, "Nooo! Mr. T-Mac is my counselor!" To stop the big problem, now I have a class, I'm a specialist and guess what? P.E class! I'm a Coach specialist. I have to read kids' file and information of families thanking us for our help. All the parents like to see their kids doing something in sports now, I feel good about that too. It looks like I have a big job to do, to have them do something new this year. Because all the parents are asking what we are going to do, well we are going to do, "Kung fu fighting! We are Kung fu fighting! Huh! Huh! Huh! Everybody Kung fu fighting! Huh! Huh! Huh!" All kids love to fight but I think what they do in class was off the hook, at first it will be two or three kids who are not feeling it so I had to think of something fast, I said, "Well, think about someone that you do not like in your mind, close your eyes and when you see them, start beating them up!" Man, I wish you could see them, their little hands are moving fast, I mean very fast and after that they feel good getting it all out.

But I tell them that there is a right time to fight, I put it down clearly. We are having fun, over time something beautiful is created, happiness means a better set of circumstances, and next, I give the kids confirmation. I make it very clear that they understand when to fight and not to fight. The danger is that we will judge the end by the beginning, or to be more exact, we will judge what we cannot see by what we can see. Do good and not evil, all things work together for the good. Let us repeat it class, they all said, "Right time to fight and a right time not to fight". So now we may truly say, have a good day kids, "Bye, Mr. T-Mac", all the kids said, let me answer the question with another question. What is your alternative?

If you don't believe in yourself, who will? I am feeling cool and confident about myself so I decided to go help Mary. "Are you keeping a close eye on me T-Mac?" "I didn't know I was suppo-" Mary cut me off, "I'm happy you're here, can you help me T-Mac?" "Yes, Mary!" "I love it when you work with me T-Mac, I do not have to tell you what to do.", "You are a good teacher Mary, other people might not think so, but the kids know more, all things work together for the good Mary." "You can say that for most of us," Mary said.

We laughed, "You're extremely pretty Mary, I have to tell you that." "Thank you," she said. I said, "You know what, as a matter of fact, black is an excellent color for the heat and you cool me off Mary, you and me only two colors, black and white we make gray together", we went on from police car, to salt and pepper for a long time, we were coming up with something funny to say, about black and white, we live in a world of frightful givens, scared to open their hearts, given that you will care about that person, no one thinks about the givens anymore. Mary and I were joking all day and it is a Beautiful thing too, not thinking about any problems. You see, I can feel it, I feel love from Mary. "Hey Mary, put a pair of gray socks in your mouth", "Hey T-Mac, put a pair of white panties in your mouth". Our jokes become sexual, and I trust that by now, we all know what will happen eventually, well if you can guess it. I'm sitting my ass on top of the water tower, looking at Malibu Beach with a hard dick. My game is not working. Stop laughing at me! I can hear you, yes you! Don't look around because I'm talking to you, yeah you!

Let's go back to the beginning. Her eyes is a beautiful ocean blue, I'm sitting here looking at the ocean, thinking about that day Mary and I were eye to eye in a heated something, I cannot explain what it was. We laughed, we joked but we have not finished that passionate day that we had, I think we went too far. We have gracefulness, this is it, my observations to answer long standing question about my passion. I would love to say we fucking gasped and wheezed on top of the water tower. You read that right! Stop thinking that we look pretty good! Yes, you said that! I want to see them up close, I want to lift up their toes and inspect their claws, and feel their skin, and open their jaws, and have a look at their teeth. Until then, I don't know for sure. But yes, they look good. Ssshhh... Hay! that's my ass! You animal! A joke on you dog! Get your nose out your ass, sshh,

I got you, well sunlight was gone, but darkness set in. It looks like it's time to take the kids. "Found it!" "Give it to me, boy! I get to use it first, Mr. Mark." "What, are you kidding?" the little man said. Did I help? Hell no! I laughed because that was me once upon a time, well for a minute, I wanted to say I'm the man! As a way to get started, I pulled the little man's chair close to mine and beat him up with my eyes. "Everybody Kung Fu fighting, huh! Huh! Everybody Kung Fu fighting huh! Huh! Huh!" "Here you go coach!" Little man said. "Thank you son" I said, "When you come to my classroom tomorrow, you can have it back. It's a nice rock!" "Thank you coach" he said. One day, he can be an anthropologist and will do a research on which came first, the rocks or the earth. They said that a rock killed all the dinosaurs.

Tomorrow is a special Olympic Day, they are all pretty and happy talking about that day, fortunately there are no losers, they are all winners. I couldn't believe my ears, that they know each other, Mary and Robin. Let me tell you, we have the kids for only two weeks then they go home, we get new kids but before the new kids come all the workers have free time, that's why I am now sitting on water tower, we are in Malibu having a good time but we cannot eat at all the restaurants in Malibu. We will have our yellow staff shirt, with a picture of a green tree on it and around it is Camp Bloomfield's staff, then we can eat at the restaurant half price, but we have to pay for alcoholic drinks if we want to have some good time. Robin found it difficult to smile back, one day, she asked me to go to beach with her and I said, "Yes Robin, I'd love to", we ended up in Tranquist Beach. Pepperdine college students' hangout there, drinking beer and smoking weed. All the white guys were giving me the bad boy look, like they were cool. I was the only black guy on the beach and it made me think why Robin asked me to come up there. She seemed to know all the guys up there, I saw a big muscled guy coming down the sand, looking at Robin like an eagle and Robin looked up to him. She walked back to me and took her clothes off, let me tell you something, she looks very simple all the time with braces on her teeth and her hair is always tied in a ponytail. But let me tell you this, the view that I saw was awesome! Damn! I love her sexy body, I mean my eyes were all on those ass, my lips were like "kiss it boy, kiss it!" She picked up her pants off the sand and put them in my hands my eyebrows rose, still thinking about that ass. My nose was telling me to smell her pants "Go, go I'm telling you, you're going to love them!", she laid her hair down, it was all going in slow motion, her long curly black hair was flowing freely, she shook her head in a very sexy way.

Man, Robin is a pretty smart woman who knows how to get a man's attention. Yes, believe me, she had me under her power, I see her like a different new woman, sexy as hell. Her light green eyes looked so beautiful, without her glasses on, she didn't look like a geek. Muscle head guy was looking at me while I was looking back at Robin's ass, I mean she was putting it there, so I can see. I tell you, I was enjoying it all because in some way I knew that all this was all about the big guy, may he is her ex-boyfriend or something. Hell, when a woman puts her sexy ass all in your face, and have some panties on, I'll be looking at her.

I was convinced that muscle head knew it too. If eyes could talk, it would have said, "Damn girl! Can I get some fries with that ass!" I'm loving it, muscles head comes over to me, and then it happened! Robin kissed me on the cheek, "Hmmm", she said in a soft voice, "I will be back T-Mac." She walks away, her ass was talking, I mean walking. It was saying "Bag that ass up, bag it up!" And she knows that all eyes are on her ass, it was like saying "Come and get me boys!" "Hey! You black guy, what's up homie! Are you seeing my girl Robin?" muscle head said. I looked at him and felt like laughing, "My name is T-Mac, well you got me on that one, she said I am"

"No! She is just mad at me" he said. "Well, I think you need to go over there and kiss her little ass and make up because before you know it, she is hooking up with a black man. You know, if she goes black she will never come back." He turns red, I was thinking, what the hell, if I fuck her, he is not getting her back. I know he is not going to fuck up because of that ass. I'm going to run, I'm not a fool! "Believe me when I say I live to fight another day", muscle head said, "You work at the camp with robin?" I said, "Well, it's a yes or no answer, It's like this, she is a counselor so they are with the kids all day and night, I'm a specialist, I have a class room, when it's her time to come to my class, we work together. I teach kung fu." I ate a forkful of pie and he went for it, his voice was softer after that and he told me to have a nice day. I can see robin and him working things out and that's what it's all about. Robin and mayor are having a good time giggling, it's like, "Man, I'm in heaven with all the beautiful women up here in Camp Bloomfield.

The counselor puts the kids in bed early today so they can wake up early for fresh warm air. Today is the big day, all the kids are going to have an excellent time. The playground sounds like there is a thunderstorm taking place for the big day, the special Olympic. There will be back to back fun, from basketball to running and swimming, you name it and we have it all. The kids are all big smiles, there are ice creams, cakes, candies, drinks and all them sweet and fatty snacks. Like my little brother will say, "my dreams all in one day", but no one is sitting around getting fat. The little people are getting their money, running fast in the playground, you can see smiles on their faces and some are blind and deaf but today they can all see and hear, they all love winning! It is a good day today for the kids and me, I said my goodbyes because they will be going home tomorrow since summer is coming to an end. I'm going to miss it up here, specially Mary, let me see what she's up to. At the horse cabin, she looked at me and wondered what I was doing as she pushed her away down to me, I stopped crying but my eyes might still be red. She said, "Are you crying T-Mac?" "Well Mary, these are tears of joy", I'm just standing here thinking "Hey, I have not seen you all day Mary."

I notice that her eyes look red too, like she has been crying, I wanted to ask her why. "I'm going to miss it up here and you all" Mary said. My eyes never leaves her face, this was the first time that I see sadness in her face like an animal locked in a cage, it is a sight that she and I are not used to. Each time I look at her, I realize that I'm falling in love with this woman. I can have a beautiful cop and I will be your handcuffed prisoner Mary, I am your best assistant horseman to make your moments happier. I want to picture her smile for a life time and laugh with her so hard about such a terrible love I have for her.

Can I live with it knowing that I never told her and it's the same every day, can she feel the power of my love? I can feel her punch knocked my heart, I see your point Mary but the only thing she thinks I'm going to miss is our friendship. I have to let her know, "I love you Mary, I always have the first day I set eyes on you", Mary turns towards me, there is just one or two things more to do, kiss and make love. It seems entirely too real to her, more real than any others who fell in love with her, the extravagant emotions of the night and the bright stars in the sky are so beautiful just like Mary's eyes. I found a new joyful beginning of a romantic love with a woman and not a girl. We kiss like there is no tomorrow, can't tell you much about how I felt but unfortunately, it was a screaming experience like I'm having a day dream. I'm telling you about it but you promise you are not going to tell anyone okay, here it goes.

My eyes were closed kissing her then she touched my body and I opened my eyes to hold her shoulders, I trailed my hands down her hips and cupped her ass, lifted her up on the hay and settled her on top of me then she was ripping off her own clothes so hastily! She was stripping down to a black bony nakedness, it was a cool move that Mary had me in. She was moving herself up and down slowly, "So tight Mary!", I was screaming, then she moves faster, she were kissing my nipples, biting down gently, throwing my head back and letting out a long, deep sigh "Ohhhh Mary". She said "Do it, T-Mac, fuck the shit out of me baby!" and she was coming and gasping for air. Her hair are all over her face, I'm coming like a mad man, but still have eyes of compassion, we had eye contact and she pinched my butt, "Oh shit," she said, "I'm not sure I'm gonna let you go home tomorrow", "You will tie me up mary? I knew you are a freek!" we laughed "I hope it was good for you as it was for me". Man, keep the salt and pepper rack because we are not eating dinner, I didn't tell you how we were eating each other out, I'm going to keep that to myself, before you really think that I'm a super freak too, she is a freak, a super freak, she is a super freak yeah… Easy right, about ten yards, easy forward, easy lift, easy right six yards, yeah! Stop right here, what is this, I'm hearing Mary does not want to see me.

I was thinking, so I went to her cabin room. I am sitting on a tree stump in front of her room thinking why is she did not say goodbye or give me her phone number so I can call her or she can call me. Cars after cars of parents picking up their kids and I am still waiting for my ride to pick me up, Mr. Gregory and my little brother, I hope I see Mary come down the steps before they get here or I'm going to knock on her door. I tried to relax my mind.

The next couple of minutes went by quickly and with agony, I have to stop thinking because I'm only making it worse and it will only make more problems. There is a gap in Mary's door so I looked up and I saw

Robin, she looked back to me. Now, it is beginning to sink in, that look was a bad sign but I am not going to say anything to Robin about Mary and me yesterday night. I carefully think about it, and they ask robin to tell me what she knows, give away a little more until the next line comes out, only hearing part of my mine, I pick up all I can from her. It took a few seconds for robin to cage her brain for whatever she is going to tell me, she swing around to head for me, she is like a beautiful butterfly! Goddamn! Who cares? Anyway Robin said, "Hey T-Mac! you all set to go home?" I said I'm ready to go up there to see Mary, "Well, T-Mac I do not think that's a good idea", I feel so down today, I can't believe that Mary is rejecting me like this after a good night of perfection time and time again. This happened to me before and probably will happen again, there really is nothing unique in what is happening in Mary's love for me. I thought, "Did I pay too little attention to the small things and too much to the big external stuff?" Am I too aggressive, overwhelming her with love? Did I set a proper example as a man and not a boy, I'm not going to allow Mary's stupidity to drive this black dick into the dirt, I'm not going to lose anymore lover or read anymore letters. "So Robin, why is Mary not seeing me?" I'm tired of listening to the same stories and Robin went over and over again, only her face changes but she never answered my question. Mary is all I am thinking as Robin keeps talking about shit. Those testimonials about Mary and her leadership, can they stop the game? I'm young, but I'm not a fool! Mary has something she's not telling me about her family, maybe because I'm black! I wondered back and forth, drifting away from Robin and Mary's cabin room.

I am sitting in front of the office on a rock looking for my boss' truck to come and pick me up when a long gray limo passes me and stops "Mary and Robin walk to the limo crying really hard with tears running down their faces.

My eyes begin to water when she looks at me, I cannot hold my tears any longer, they run down my face and Mary runs towards me and kisses me so passionately but quietly. I whispered in her ear "I love you!" And she cried even more. I told her to call me, she whispered back, "T-Mac, when you think you have it all figured out, something will always go wrong." I don't know where all the pieces fit in this big jigsaw puzzle of love for a woman like Mary.

When it all comes to an end, you need to welcome a brand new day. Boys in the hood always come talking like trash knowing nothing in life but to be legit. Don't quote me boy because I am saying shit. Back to the project life, shit are still the same as always, a funeral for someone getting killed by the hands of an enemy or his friends for the love of money. I'm seeing new faces for the four months that I was gone, it's funny how people can adapt to their environment. The ghetto nigga out here are getting their papers, for dope you can call it snow white, everybody has their own corner. The pusher, the crack head, and the hoes have their corners and the policemen know the hood just like us.

I'm sitting here thinking about hell, I'm back in hell and shit are still the same but there are new faces that live in the ghetto now. Is this shit going to b my life? I laughed because I was missing it, well hell, I was becoming a geek in Malibu over time but a geek's life is not so bad if I think about it with a big smile on my face. Yes, I said it but don't quote me boy, because I am saying shit, ha, ha, ha. I live in the grave yard, so I know you are not talking shit. Well, you see me back to my old self, I mean, if you like to live here in the project you have to be hard. I see this hoe moving fast my way, well my house is in the corner where all the pushers hang out, she has paper clutched in one hand. Before, she always wears soft pinkish lipstick and just a small touch but this morning, her lipstick is thick and fire red like the color of a fire truck.

A hoe's life is violence and rough sex, the pimp kicks that ass for spinning her money with a dope pusher, she changed her hair as well, still looks beautiful but now she is more like the witch queen in the movie, Snow white. All the dope slanger knows that this hoe has money in her hands and by the way she is walking so fast, she has cash. All the pushers get her attention shouting out their ass, they are hiding in trees and grasses so the policeman cannot get their shit or go to jail for it. A fight! He is getting his ass kicked, he is saying "I told your bitch ass you cannot sell on this corner if you are not working for me." Yeah, that's life here, communication is a step closer to the grave, when your life is hash in your face, and someone will say "no time!" That means cops, if you know what I mean. I look up the street and I noticed a white chevy van, which to me, doesn't fit in the neighborhood like a perfect puzzle piece. At the back, two cops are making movies through the dark windows, the guy that was beating up the other guy runs over to my side of the alley and he hides under an ash tree, right beside me. He said, "Yeah, you are that Jehovah's witness boy huh?" I knew I have sinned having sex without marriage with two persons, and one is a married woman who I'm still in love with that keeps running over and over in my mind. If I knew that Mary is married, would I still make love with her passionately knowing she has a husband?

A husband who loves her truly, would I still fuck her? My mind is so fucked up right now. I looked the thug in the eyes and said, "Well, my mom is, I used to be one." He saw the darkness in my eyes and he likes to say that I'm one of them, I mean from the look on his face it's got to be serious that I did some fuck up shit not to be a witness any more. "Hey homie! They call me Lil Ice." "I'm Turtle!" "Ha!ha!ha Turtle?!" he said, "I like you kid, the turtle beats the rabbit!" The cops have one of the dope slanger handcuffed and one cop talks to the hoe. "Damn!" Lil Ice said, "I told that nigga to stop keeping that shit in his ass. He's a parolee, damn it! Hey Turtle, let's walk homie, let me treat you to some ice cream." Something is telling me to say "Hell no!" But in the ghetto, the word "free" does not come around all the time. "Turtle", Lil ice said on the way to the ice cream truck. I always think about the old man, the cool ice cream man, someone killed him, that's fuck up! "It's like this, I'm going to put you on hell of a game turtle nigga! I know your ass needs money so I'm going to help you youngster, but do not fuck me man so I do not have to fuck you up, understand Turtle?!" "Hey, big players! What's going down? Help your brother here.", Lil ice said, "Get your nasty ass out of here, you want to be a pimp ass out of my face? Your punk ass is not getting shit from me" Lil ice said, "Oh nigga, where's your bitch at? That hoe owed me money, tell her ass to get my money or I'm going to fuck both of you up man. Slick rick is getting his ass on talking shit, saying that's why I didn't work for your ass in a run wall that shit was funny", Lil ice said, "it's a dog eats dog world Turtle. To have more, you must have a heart that only the strong survives." He hated his heart, living it in the most dangerous way did push me because I'm close to the edge. I'm trying not to lost my head yeah, mommy and daddy do not know their baby is having moonneeyy! I'm the man! The corner was a mess, all hoes loved to get some of me. "I'm here cutie pies, Oh well I'm there Lil' sexy pie" I don't say it but these hoes play with the game nigga. If you hate niggas, I will put my Smith and Wesson in your mouths. Why is the nigga put in handcuffs? I was making them pigs eat my dust. Hell, I knew running shit is going to come in good hands, well I can say I was a geek all the time but mirror, mirror on the fucking wall, who is the fucking baller in this ghetto of them all?! ICE FROST! What the fuck happened to Lil ice? Well, you can say that's what his ass is, LITTLE Ice! I'm the Big MACK, you get it? Let me stop talking like the joker in riddles, that nigga was fucking me for my paper. Hell yes, my ass was making money! No job can pay me the stack of money in my shoe boxes.

Lil ice and I had a gun fight, I beat his ass, and then bitch ass nigga ran got his gun. I layed his ass down when the cops came, he was right there in his own blood laying on the ground with his gun in his hand. Well, it opened up old murder cases, the gun connected to the crime victims who lived, you know the shot, and his ass is gone for good.

Well I have been ducking my ass off, I fuck all the sexy bitches in the projects. Oh, let me tell you this. Well, let Michelle tell you, "Nigga, I don't know why the hell is your ass not in college. I'm hearing shit about your ass around this project, your ass is still Turtle to me. You call yourself T-Mac, hell, boy your ass cried like a baby about that white bitch you fucked up at that camp Bloom. You know what the fuck I'm talking about. I told you, your ass likes those white girls like that half bitch Gigi. That bitch looked white to me nigga! I gave you game about them bitches and now you are having all those hoes going crazy nigga. I gave you all your first black pussy nigga. I fuck the shit out of your ass, you know I did nigga! Your ass said, Michelle I Love you and I like to keep our friendship, Hell nigga! You are still fucking those project hoes. Why are they still blowing up your cell phone nigga, the mac! Nigga, you hitting this pussy tonight, friends my ass! Oh Turtle, I heard what you did to that Gigi bitch, nigga you are crazy!" "Well, you see Michelle, I'm going to put up one game with me, but keep it to yourself okay? This is the truth, that bitch ass Gigi came to the projects about three months after Camp Bloomfield, she came to show off her new red scooter that she sold me out for. Well in the 80's you are a baller if you had one, and Gigi is showing her ass off, "Hey T-Mac", "What's up Gigi?"

"Nothing much T-Mac, I see your ass is not going to college. You look like a crack-head, I see that you are hanging with them now."

I started to flush, I know this bitch shouldn't come in my hood talking shit on my corner! I'm the man and she is calling me a crack-head, thinking that she is the shit because she has a new scooter that she sold me out for? I reached and pulled my 9 millimetre and shoot the tires on her scooter. I walked off and went to my low rider, sat in my car and saw her pushing her scooter down the street. I drove by her real slow playing my song, "La, da, da, de, da, da, da, da, da, da, daaa! Everybodys got a little groove, under the light, under the light, under the light, it's! T-Macccc!" As the song said my name, I turned it up, her mouth fell open. My low rider was the shit. I know you're saying I'm cold brother for doing that to Gigi, well I told you a brother adapts to his environment and if you like hanging with me, you need to have the heart. Welcome to the ghetto, well I can say, that bitch Lil ICE put me up on game. It's like this, that nigga sent his boys after me, yeah the nigga tried to kill me from behind bars. I was doing my thing making my paper on the block when I heard slick rick screaming, "Get out of the fuckin' street T-Mac!" I looked and saw a four door Cadillac come down the street with head lights off.

When it got close, I saw pistol out the car window and someone said, "You're a dead sonofabitch!" with this, I turned and ran to the building. I heard a series of gun shots, I ran my ass off, not to win a race but to save my life. I crossed the sidewalk to the building, I looked at them and I saw them turned around. I had my pistol out now, there were people shouting in the hallway. They are coming back, I'm going to let them mofuckers have it so I timed their ass, one second, two, three! They let off boom! Boom! One of the niggas in the car was screaming "Stop! Stop!" I think I get his ass banged up, I pop up several shots through the front car door, I said, "Fuck you asshole! die, die asshole!" He shot three more times! "You dumb sonofabitch, T-Mac", Slick Rick shouted, "get the fuck out here T-Mac!" I backed up looking at the car, turned and ran to the apartment building and down the hill to the front door of the building to my sexy baby Kim's fucking apartment.

My heart was pumping fast, "What's happening? What's happening?" My girl asked me, "Nothing baby, go back to sleep. The niggas outside are just being niggas". "Goodnight. sleep well baby" Kim said. "I'm happy you are not out in that bullshit baby. I will be happy when I finish this nursing school so we can get out of the projects because I do not want anything to happen to you baby." Man, I had that dream before, I feel uncomfortable, but she did not need to know. I was in the deep, I mean my pistol was still smoking hot under her bed. I lay my arms around my baby Kim thinking who have a hit out for me, I have no enemy that I know of. The federal entry team and the Los Angeles teams stabilized the area and bust the other tenant out of the apartment building and the adjacent building that Slick Rick said the gunman went to. Well, two niggas died in the car, can you believe this shit, one of the niggas was Lil' Ice's cousin so I sent his ass my condolence. "Dear Lil ICE, you know I never would have believed you would do this. I thought you were too smart for that shit, if you'd come at me with your boys, take some time to think it over. Oh my bad, that's all you have, time to think about it huh? Well, you think it over to yourself. I sent you five thousand dollars because I heard that in prison they do not get you enough tissue to wipe your cheeks and I know you need to cry so I sent five thousand dollars so you can buy yourself some tissue. I know you are going to need some, to clean your ass too. Oh, if some new niggas come to your cell, I sent them to say hi." No return address, well yes, that nigga gave me the game, but I am the man in this project, my money is a tree and I water my tree every day. Get your paper! Man, well you see, the game doesn't stop to get your money man! Mirror on the wall, who is the man of them all? Ice frost! I shot Lil Ice's ass and he went to jail, I have to hook up with and new dope connection and Ice Frost is the man. I get up in the morning look in my big mirror to see how fresh I am, I tell myself I'm going to have my cash Like Ice Frost. I went to his apartment, it's an old building, they still have the original solid oak or walnut doors or something. By the time the apartments get this old, a crack head or another has usually stripped out all the original doors and sell them. They're probably worth as much as the apartment building. In Ice Frost's living room, there are two rickety occasional chairs, a recliner with a stained fabric cover, the brown metal cube of an aging color television, two blue vinyl bean bag chairs lay on the wooden floor. The apartment smelled like dog and weed, there is a white pit bull sitting on top of one bean bag chair, red nose pet named Cocaine. Ice frost's body looks like he did some time before the light shined. The brother has eyes of a killer, I have been fucking with him for six month and I saw him smile only once. He's always playing a chess game on the table set up, he calls it the game of life. Man, Ice frost has a way to show you the dope game, well, I think Cocaine, his pit bull likes the way he demonstrates what the power of crack cocaine can make you do. There was a young crack head at Ice frost's house, she did not look all that bad looking, Ice frost told me, "this is why you never get high on your own supply". He calls his dog Cocaine and somehow that dog knew he was going to get his dick sucked. Ice frost told the crack head girl to suck the dog's dick and that hoe went to work on Cocaine. Someone knocked on the door, Ice frost opened the door and it was crack head man who came in the living room. He saw the hoe still sucking the dog's dick, Ice frost told the hoe to give Cocaine some pussy and that nasty hoe fucked the dog! Ice frost said, "You see this shit Mac", I said, "Hell yeah", Ice frost said, "Get up hoe, get up!" He told the crack head dude to fuck that bitch. Man! He just saw this hoe fucking the dog, and now he is fucking her! Ice frost said, "Both of you, take this shit and get the fuck out of my house." It looked like a ten dollar rock, man! The power of rock cocaine. "T-Mac!" Ice Frost said, "never fuck with this shit T-Mac. I like you kid, I'm going to put you up in the big leagues, no more corn serving for you. Oh T-mac, I heard you lay that nigga Lil' Ice's folk down. That nigga was fucking with me too but his ass always come up short all the time, when I give his ass the shit, he will say, this person owes me and that person. Mac, I don't want to hear that shit mofucker! Where's my money at Mac, you never give a crack head some dope on consignment, NO MONEY! No dope!" After the game Ice frost laced me on how money was rolling in, I had the project cracking, no more corner serving for me, niggas call me for my hook ups. Oz'a only two to three keys a day, I was douge fresh, no more shoe boxes! I had to buy a safe to keep my money in and Ice frost was showing me the game of life. Hell! He always checkmates me in the game of chess, he always said, "to win you have to think three moves ahead of time Mac, that goes for the dope game too, the pigs and the jacks, you always have to outthink your opponents to be on top of the game, to win.

"That goes for the street life and this chess game T-mac, I'm going to make you a cold player Mac, those project niggas cannot fuck with this game I'm giving you. One thing Mac, never fuck the hand that feeds you mac!" Ice frost said with the eyes of a killer, when he looks at me, I knew that he is not playing when he said that to me. I put on my game face too and I said, "You don't have to worry about me Ice frost, I'm going to be your right hand man", I said to Ice frost. "Hell nigga!" Ice frost said, "do I look like your brother's keeper? I'm a businessman, money is always first, I know your ass is feeling like a new jack city nigga! You need no friends in this business, it's all about the money and don't you forget that Lil nigga!" I said to myself, Ice frost looked like the devil when he said that to me, it's one thing I knew that mom always said, "Read your Bible boy", and that shit Ice frost said didn't come from new jack city movie, it was when Cain talked to God and the Lord said unto Cain, "Where is Abel, your brother?" And Cain said, "I know not. Am I my brother's keeper?" I saw That shit in the movie and they showed Nino Brown blow his brains out and said "Know you're not!" That was moving and I deeply felt emotional for it stresses strong emotion and is related to my stimulation and inspiration. That shit is not going to happen to me but something is telling me not to trust Ice frost's ass. Well, I'm going to keep it below 100%, I will get my money and get out of the game man! That's what it's all about right? A nigga like that, I don't need for a friend, he's not to be trusted at all. I believe my ass will be in too deep and it's going to be the death of me. Trust my ass, all that niggas to me are my trust fund, especially money and securities. I mean, the project niggas look up to Ice frost because he's the man and by me being his boy, these niggas are not going to try any bullshit on me. The last nigga that Jacked Ice frost, oh boy. Well, it's like this, it's been two years ago and that nigga sister kept coming around here saying "if you guys see my little brother John, tell him to come home, that he has a family who still loves him." That bitch does not know that her brother was a jacker and Jack the wonder mofucker, and his bitch ass is dead. Some people always sit a red light looking for a notion or a light intervention or a play of the mind through fancy free, carefree, thinking her brother is still alive without commitment or restriction, she was unattached to the thought that her brother is dead. Man! Life sometimes can be a bitch huh, waiting on the light to change green, to draw a line around life's pain and hurt. To have hope is one of the conditions we all face, attending ourselves to an event and having some bearing upon it. Beyond willful control, a victim of circumstance, that's the life of a hustler on the damn street corner in the projects, that's the shit that goes along with making your money player. And if you do not have a heart for this, it's not for you, believe me. This shit sometimes fuck with your head man! Not knowing if your ass is coming back home when you step out of your door, you do not promise to come back home player. Well, I inhaled deeply on the thought, as long as Ice frost's ass is around to keep the jacker off my ass. Well, that nigga has gotten me through some pretty bad time and I immediately encountered the same chill ruffles all over my body, then my memory came rushing back not to trust Ice frost for any shit, but making my money. Frantically, my mind raced as I tried to piece together what I am going to do if something happened to this nigga's dope while it's in my hands, that nigga will kill me, I know it! He will crash down on my head for that shit. Man, the projects have it going on traffic after traffic of cars coming to the hood. This crack cocaine Ice frost gave me are the shit, the crack heads said, "T-Mac, keep this shit man, this is the best you ever had man."

Money is falling out of the sky, I had twenty two keys and that shit is gone and niggas blowing up my cell phone. The hood is on fire, the cops know there's a new man running shit in the project, I sold my low rider, it was gaining too much heat my way. Hell, I'm becoming too sexy for that car, you feel me nigga! A big daddy, hell it's been ten months. I had the project lock down, well I know I said that when I get my pager right, I'm getting out the game, but keep it real nigga, can you just walk away from $60,000 a day? Hell nah! Ice frost and I were getting along fine, well you know, I keep putting thousands in his hands, that nigga moved out of his old apartment and now living in the hills somewhere. I always have to wait for his ass to come meet me at jack in a box, "What's up Mac?", Ice frost said, "who your friend?" "Hi, my name is Sally!" she said. "What's your name?" "They call me Ice frost, baby girl", and she had a big smile on her face. Ice frost was getting his mask on, and Sally was eating it up.

"T-mac!" Ice frost said, "Is this your Girl Mac?"

I said, "I do not know that girl, I'm sitting here waiting for you, her and I are shooting the shit, you know, not talking about shit".

"Man!" Ice frost got her hook up, "Homie! She is not one of my bitches", she was looking hard to see if we are talking about her.

"Ice frost, I'm going to get the shit out of your car."

"Mac"! Ice frost said, "where your car at?"

"O", I said, "I sold it man, I'm in my girl Kim's car."

"That's right Mac", Ice frost said. I know I should not ask if the shit was the same, Ice frost is saying always so pretty, always so fun when the shit is good! And I know it's on! I realize Ice frost hooks me up this time, the bag is bigger than always. I put it in my girl's car and went back in the jack in a box. I can see Ice frost trying to calculate her age now, she said, "No! Guess again", their eyes met, he looks puzzled so Sally said, "I'm only in my mid twenty". Ice frost said, "You certainly doesn't look like it", and Sally said, "I'm twenty five Ice frost". I took a look at Sally, she is pretty, but the question to ask her is "Where your man at?" Hell! I know someone is kissing her ass. "What's up Sally" I said, "I know you have a home girl for me". Sally said, "Well yes and no, T-mac! You call yourself a mac, and you do not have a girlfriend" "I'm going to level with you Sally", I said, "I have bitch, I'm a hood nigga, women cannot keep a player like me kissing there ass". She starts giggling and had a big smile on her face, I keep on hitting her with cap, "As you see Sally, I'm a player so deep that only those who contain a player game have the same burning passion such as mine, can you see it Sally?" "Well, Mac", Sally said, "You say it like that, I do have someone for you. I think you will love her ass, she thinks she is the shit! The Miss player of the year!" I said, "Is she crazy? Sally! I like hood bitches, not crazy bitches!" Sally laughed and said, "I think you will be interested in her", I said, "Is she your cousin-by-the-dozen or is she just your friend, because you know she might be a little off." Sally could not stop giggling after that one, Ice frost looks cool as always, and he said, "Well, hook it up Sally for the night. Call me, here is my cell phone number." "Okay guys", Sally said. "If Sally will hook me up with an ugly bith in this supposed to be date, I'm not fucking with her Ice frost, you and Sally and that ugly bitch go on a date", I started to laugh. Ice frost said, "Hell no T-mac! Your ass is going to. Your ass better hope her ass looks good, oh yeah that shit you get is on flight, them niggas are going to be on your ass for that shit, so kick back today, we are going to do some fucking tonight. You know that's thirty-two birds you have that will hold you until a week T-mac!"

"Cool!" Ice frost said to me with a look of total astonishment across his face, and then he emitted a whoop of delight that stopped the buzz of conversations in Jack in a Box around us. All these years, it lingers in my memory that Ice frost discovered the scent of joy. I never thought I'd see that smile again! How is this dreadful man, I was thinking with a slight smile, besides it's always been in the back of my mind, that I'm the only friend Ice frost have, he can pay that businessman shit on someone new to the game. That nigga knows I have his back as well as I think he have mine, believe me it's true. I've lost a number of good friends lately in this dope game, because those fools think that a brother is posted to look out all the time! Hell, nigga! I'm not laying down fucking your bitch and having kids, to hell with them you little bad ass. Well, I can say each loss hurts a little more than the last friend, it's getting a bit lonely on top, absolutely lonely not knowing who you can trust, some may find it crazy.

"What's up Kim! I know, them niggas are blowing up my phone baby but I'm not doing shit tonight Kim, Ice frost asked me to help his ass do some shit for him tonight so do not open the door for anyone, home girl and all, you hear me Baby?" "Yeah, I hear you", Kim said. "I'm going to be out all night Kim", "What the fuck is Ice frost and your ass up to Baby?" Kim said. She changes her mood so fast, "Baby, you know I love your ass so stop asking me shit that you know I'm not going to tell".

It is starting to get late that afternoon, the sun is about to set and I could already feel a slight chill seeping through the poorly insulated back wall. I am about to leave the kitchen when my cell phone rings. "Hello! What's up T-mac!" Ice frost said, "get your ass outside Mac" When I went outside, I saw Sally, "Mac!" Sally said, "this is your homegirl." "Hi sweetheart!" she said, I stopped talking to feast my eyes on her, she is so beautiful. "What's your name?" I said, "Who? Me? Oh, all my friends call me Sexy V", she said. "Sexy V?! Why the hell would someone call someone as ugly as Sexy V?" Sally said laughing, "T-Mac, you are so funny! Sexy V is not ugly". Sexy V was looking at me all crazy. "You see Sally! I told you she is crazy", I said. Then sexy V said "I know you are calling me ugly nigga!" I smile at her and said, "You look so cute when you are mad Sexy V. Thank you Sally, I like her and she has one of the beautiful smiles I ever set my eyes on."I knew all her life people always call her beautiful, well not me! To tell you the truth, that's my name Pops always call me, "Damn not me!" When I did shit. Ice frost said, "I'm going to my house, I have a big screen TV and all the new movie that came out and we can order pizza and they have other shit, you can order too Sally. Well, you know what's up." "Yeah! Ice frost, a bitch knows what's up. Where do you live at Ice frost, because your ass has been on this fucking Go freeway for a long time. Hell! Where is your ass going to?" Sally said. "Yeah, Ice frost!" Sexy

V said cutting Sally off from her conversation. Ice frost said, "Just chill ladies, I live in Chino Hills, we are almost there. Sit back, we are going to have a good time." "Hey Ice frost!" Sally said, "stop and get some drinks!" "Baby girl", Ice frost said, "I have all the best shit you can buy at my house". "Damn! Ice frost", Sexy V said "Are you balling too, huh? Your ass is doing something Ice, because you are in a 1986 600S Mercedez Benz! And live in Chino Hills too! Hey bitch! Where you meet his nigga at?" Sally laugh but did not say any shit knowing that Sexy V is trying to come on to Ice frost. I was saying to myself Sexy V is a cold Bitch like Sally, said…

That is a long march to madness, all this shit going on in this car, it feels good to get off that mother fucking freeway. I'm looking out the car window at the mountain standing ominous and alone, it looks taller than it was, and the growl outside turns lighter as the sun goes down behind Chino Hills. Damn! We are going to this big ass' driveway, the girls are not saying shit and my ass too. I am playing it off so cool, like saying this ain't shit, I'm not a player heating Ice frost, I'm acting like I come here all the time, well you know this is my shit too. You feel me, this bitch Sexy V will fuck the shit out of a brother, damn right! I'm a cold nigga too, this bitch Sexy V thinks she has game ha! Ha! Ha! Well, me too. The homie Ice shit is fat! My precision is that the dining area, a red-orange and blue wall serves as a reminder of Steven Shortridge's complex design scheme. When the glass doors slide into a pocket wall, the division between the front courtyard and the kitchen disappears. Man! Ice frost's shit is off the hook. A big wide screen TV fit for a king, black leather love sets, and the walls have photographs of works of Art from black heroes. The Architect who did this shit did his thing really well. I looked out at the back, damn! This nigga has a well lighted pool and a tennis court with a three-stall horse paddock and direct. Ice frost has a helly! His house is an award winner, it has five bedrooms and six bathrooms in a 7, 469 square feet lot and a view overlooking Chino City! This is the kind of living I'm talking about! You know what I mean? This nigga has housekeepers too!

Me and Ice frost are not so close in some aspects, and yet so distant with others. All my old friends fell off but Ice frost and I remain relative strangers. How would you characterize our relationship, friendship or just business? I know our connection is all about that damn page! That mofucking money man, dollars, dollar bills y'all! To pay for a house like this one, nigga you better believe that shit, Ice frost and I are playing a game of chess, and this chess set is a royal diamond chess set, I mean some displays of wealth are just outrageous, but the polished mahogany board compliments the diamond accents and handcrafted 18-karat white-and-yellow gold pieces. Nigga! If your money is that much, put your mouth on your money or consider this the ultimate stage for the nigga town gamble and this mofucking chess set is a special order at $200,000! So you like to gamble huh? Drop your cash or shut up because your broke ass is checkmate! I am looking at Sexy V and Sally watching the widescreen TV and on their cellular phones. Women only do that shit, because when Kim asks to rent movies, I cut my shit off. They made themselves comfortable and propped pillows behind their backs and they were on the phone for nearly two hours, I know because Ice frost and I have been playing chess game for that long and this nigga got $10,000 from my pocket already. I didn't come all the way out here for this nigga to fully illustrate he's the king, not to impose upon Ice frost's game, but I only come out here to fuck these bitches. I have to say this ticket admit the whole group but what I'm saying is, all are asses, I got other shit in my mind, like the girls who are on their fucking phones all the time, this nigga Ice frost's ass, and this mofucking chess set that costs more than his 600.S Mercedes Benz. He's an ass thinking that I'm going to pay for that shit. Hell! Shit is already $10,000 it is absolutely over for me, you can believe that shit from my ass, Hell! You know like I said, I came to fuck this bitch's ass. I'm looking at her ass right now, legs open with that fat ass pussy, damn that shit looks good. "What's up Sexy V, why don't you get off that damn phone and tell that nigga you will call him back, I got to holla at you". She had a glass or two of wine, she was feeling herself acting like she has a deep emotion for who she holla at on the phone, and Sally said, "T-mac! Stop fucking with her, she is talking to her people nigga, are you tripping?" I said, "I already told both of you to stop acting like a pair of schoolgirls on their phones, putting little spells in nigga's minds lying your ass off." Well, nothing changes, I still think that both of these bitches are crazy and that's not an infatuation.

Sally is always a giggly bitch laughing at all my jokes. Well, sometimes I do have an amusing story or a mischievous trick and prank for them, I am always the laughing stock of the party, well, not today but something is telling me that the two of them are really very close even if Sally is acting like she hardly kicks it with her when I ask her this morning for a home girl hook up. Looking at them now, it seems to be beyond what has been said about her friendship with Sexy'V. Oh, that bitch Sexy'V is still outside talking to that nigga on her phone, Sally said it's her people, ha!ha!ha! Who are these bitches fooling? Oh shit! Ice frost and Sally are going up the marble staircase, the entrance to the stairs are overwhelmingly large. This house is breathtaking and Sally knows it too that's why that hoe is going upstairs with Ice frost to give up some ass thinking that she will be moving in here. Well, this is a bold undertaking advice, Ice frost is getting some action, I acknowledge that shit! Why is my ass still sitting here with a hard dick while this bitch Sexy'V is still outside talking to that fool on the phone?

Fuck! Something is telling me to call my girl Kim to this nigga house, damn it! Ice frost owes me for this bullshit. As I was thinking all of these, Sexy'V's ass walked back in the house. This bitch is sexy, "Hey T-mac!" Sexy'V said, "I apologize, I was talking to my mom, she has my son. You know how boys can be sometimes, well Jame is my baby daddy, he is coming over here tripping and saying that he is taking his son from me! That nigga is not doing shit, his ass doesn't have a job, and hasn't done one thing for his son! He is just mad because I'm not fucking with his ass anymore. Hell! That nigga still lives at home with his mama!" I was saying to myself, she is real at the moment but that nigga can still fuck her ass. I don't need no damn approximation, women sometimes process themselves. I mean, she is fucking the man and having a relationship and the brother has a big setback you know, your ass is broke and your bitch or your nigga, kicks rock at you and the kids and all, but when shit gets back to money, you know, having a great deal of money, he or she will be back fucking the shit out of you and you will think that the sex is good because they love you. Hell! Where's your ass at because I can use some money too! That is unbeknownst, I have been looking for one like that, girl where are you? All the bitches are players without knowing shit, Hell! Ladies are like some niggas too, the game is to be sold not told, you feel me? Man, I didn't expect Sexy'V to hold my hand, well the whole time she was running her mouth busy talking about baby mama drama. Besides that annoying story, I hope Sexy'V accommodate my ass in a new surrounding, like up those damn stairs and give me some of that fat ass pussy! I can't stop looking at it all this time, this bitch is running her deep emotion over nothing. I give a shit about Sexy'V's cellular phone ringing, she picks up the phone. "Hello?" Sexy'V said! "Nigga I told you my mama is not going to open up the door for your ass!" She hangs up the phone and said, "T-mac I'm cutting my shit off, fuck that nigga!" I said, "I'm glad to see that you look a bit happier Sexy'V". "Yeah!" she said, "I'm not going to let that nigga fuck up my night T-mac, a bitch needs some dick, what's up nigga!" I am all smiles because she is pretty, I reached for her hand lifting it to her face, moving it slowly caressing her cheek and chin, but there is no question that I am getting no pussy, she might seem annoying at times, but hell, all women are yes a brother loves to delight them. I can say for most nigga, it's just that I want to help her you know, this shit doesn't come around that frequently when a sexy ass bitch tells you to fuck the shit out of her and believe me, I'm not having any bitter disappointment about this shit, it is a relief with my hard dick that needs some pussy, you feel me player?! I'm looking at her in the eyes laying in a king size bed in my arms, her body is so sexy! I'm beginning to see why her friends call her Sexy'V, she has a great ass and that monkey is fat with no hair on it and her pussy is shining and juicy. I had my finger up it, playing in her fat ass monkey, kissing her, but she has no passion in her eyes, and just receiving, she is very passive without responding to the heated moment. Hell! I was thinking, we are not in love or anything, we are just fucking so I'm cool with that. As soon as I am about to stick my shit in, I hear a gunshot. Damn! Ice frost must be happy already because he fuck the shit out of Sally's ass and he is showing off his guns, but fuck that! "I'm going to see what's up Sexy'V, okay?" I open the bedroom door and I can see Ice frost laying in the hallway floor bleeding like a mofucker with blood coming out of his mouth. "Oh shit!" I said, "hold on Ice frost! Hold on man! I'm going to call for an ambulance, just hold on man!" I got the gun out of his right hand thinking that I'm going to kill that bitch Sally. I'm looking at Ice frost, standing over him with his gun in my hand thinking about getting some ass resisted, and Ice frost seems to have forgotten to endure how to live. It must be painful, nevertheless he has no place for repentance, though he fought it diligently with tears and his head flopped to the floor. I hear a gun sound "Click! Click!" I look up and see a nigga in black ski mask, one of the mofucker's gun jammed, he was trying to fix it while the other two had their guns pointed at my face. Nigga said, "Drop the gun nigga! Drop it Now!" All this shit is going in slow motion in my mind, first, the two bitches Sally and Sexy'V who acted like they were not bestfriends. Hell! I knew that shit was a lie, you can just feel it when Sally stands up for Sexy'V about that fucking phone call saying that it's her people and Sexy'V went outside so she could unlock the front door and the niggas call her back to see if she has done it talking in code, making me believe that it was her baby daddy at her mom's house and when she said that she is not going to open the door it actually meant that the door is unlocked. These bitches played on Ice frost and me, "Nigga! You don't hear me? Drop the mofucking gun!! Drop it!" I cannot believe this shit is going down, Ice frost lying on the floor. "Die man! My nigga die!!" I know these punk ass niggas are going to kill me too so I raised my gun and shot, Click! Click! Daammn!!! Boom, Boom Boom!!!

I tried to open my eyes but it takes a lot of effort, my head hurts so much. "Where am I?" I immediately encountered a soft like surface changed, hold up! This is too satire, instinctively I screamed until I was hoarse, until I couldn't scream anymore, I can hear the sound of bells, but there was nothing but silence. I listen, hoping to hear something but there is only silence, darkness and silence. I'm truly alone, I had to keep calm, I couldn't let this shit overwhelm me, but how? How did this shit happen? Then I remembered, I'm going to kill them bitches and niggas, then I hear sound of bells ringing again, a combination of...

The Dr. said, "Come on people! We are losing him!" beep...beep... beeeeep.....! Something muffled the sound, I can't hear them, then I felt myself searching in order to find something, overhead a mound of revival, I was not prepared for this shit man! A raw earth shimmered in the light of fire, behind me was pure darkness, How did I get here? Then I saw a door of fire, the door is on fire! I can see people dancing, but death ran all around it. But I'm alive! I can hear them screaming! My eyes opened and stared in terror into the absolute cardinal red fire, I was unable to move any farther, then he comes, and... Oh, my God! It's Ice frost!! He has horns on his head! Oh shit, he's the devil, he has a tail, cloven hoofs, he's satan, the ruler of hell and foe of God! I'm alive! I'm screaming I'm alive... I need to be alive! A big burst of flame came around me, I was dancing a macabre of pain. The Devilish Ice frost makes me do my own destruction.

He keeps saying, "You want the shit! You get the shit!! The he laughs hur… hur…hur…! I scream then my eyes open, I am in a hospital bed and there's a nurse standing next to me, she said "Baby, you are having a bad dream, it's okay sweetheart, you need something for pain!" I said, "Is my friend who came in with me all right? He was shot too!". "Mr. Tmac!" the nurse said, "I don't know what you are talking about being shot baby, you are in the hospital for pneumonia! You are really sick but I'm here to help you okay? If you need something, tug on the string. Now try to get some good sleep and have an open charitable mind so the nightmares will go away." "Thank you", I said. Oh, it feels good to find someone to talk to. Then my memory comes rushing back, I laughed immediately because I realized that all this shit is a dream.

Well, do you remember when I was playing Eazy E song "Boys in the hood that always hard!" I remember lying down in bed at home playing that song, I was not feeling so good because I just came back from, you know Camp Bloomfield. I must have gotten sick, when my I sit on top of the water tower all night crying about Gigi and what coach did to me and maybe that's how I got this pneumonia. I remember having my first nightmare killing little ice people with a new Smith & Wesson and my little brother Anthony woke me up saying, "Michelle is here for you", and Michelle said, "What's up Turtle! You look fucked up! I heard what Coach and that bitch Gigi did. Why has your ass haven't been coming to school? But you know, I'm going to put you up on game! Oh those bitches will lose in the state meet ha!ha!ha! Fuck them Turtle! You have scholarship, I mean a scholarship!"

You see, the day of the scholarship assembly, I was on top of the water tower at Camp Bloomfield crying about, I decided to retire and get away from it all. Michelle said, "Why are you not smiling nigga? Forget about coach and Gigi, Turtle"! I can see you are not in a good mood." Well, you see, it's not that I was not in a good mood that day, I was sick! Well you know, the fucking pneumonia. But that day that Michelle talked to me, I thought I was having a daydream and I must have fallen back to sleep and dreamt about Michelle getting on me about liking white girls and she gave me my first black pussy and I fucked her over Gigi's red scooter and then I killed Lil Ice's cousin. Lil Ice was the nigga that gave me a game, I shot his ass up and he when to jail so I had to hook up with a new dope connection, which was Ice frost Satan the Devil himself, damn!

My ass is laughing about all this fucking dream. I'm happy for that shit, but the only thing I'm not so happy about is my broke ass laying in this hospital bed. I can't even rub two pennies together, I'm broke is hell. Well, it's better than being in Hell! Oh, nightmare, a brother is laying here in this bed with a hard dick and no girlfriend! Well, in my dream I had one, you remember her? Man, she was beautiful! Yes, Kim was a black queen who lived in the projects attending nursing school. That is the only thing that's good in that nightmare and that dumb T-mac was going to fuck over her for a sexy ass hood rat named Sexy'V. Take it from me brothers, we all do some fucked up shit to destroy our relationships, well, I can say in real life I don't know why Gigi fucked over my heart like she did but I still love her. Someone stole her heart away from me, it's just me and I in my head and no one need to know Gigi!

You know, sometimes life overindulges us excessively, having too much gratification and being unwise, and what more shall I say for the time that you fail? I will tell you that your heart is sitting at a red light, be happy for the present even if it is painful, nonetheless, afterwards you will yield peace, love and righteousness and will strengthen the heart which hangs down, and before you know it, the light is green and you will fall in love again, who knows? But believe me, let us lay aside every weight of love pain, or errors to commit a sinful act on your ex- lover which so easily ensnares us and let us run with endurance the race that is set before us, the traffic light! It's 100 miles and running, my life is like a traffic light, it's stops and goes all the time even when shit doesn't go right! together, stop crying! It's time to celebrate. I feel good, I mean inside this damn hospital I feel like a drug addict, their fucking narcotic shit is good! I'm high like a motherfucker! That sweet old nurse lady became a bitch! Well, you got me, I tug on that string when I said, "Bitch where my shit at? And you can give me the shot in my ass to kill all of my pain". And that's what I see in the people in the projects, they drown their troubles away by drinking until they get drunk, the unattested variant of drugs. Yes it may offer some help, like a dry run, test your heart by exercising in bombing up your drink and attacking yourself to other combat skills without the use of live ammunitions in a bottle!

You remember this, the professor Alcoholic, a physical ghetto anthropologist who did a research on trying to figure out which come first: the bottle or the alcohol! You agree huh? Life sometimes can move backwards, having knowledge or information about someone about your acquaintanceship, the person who only knows your pillow talk and when they get mad at you, they will put all your shit in the streets, damn! Do you hear that shit? I do, well, it's a risk and you know that running your mouth can sometimes backfire at your ass. Let us go and do where we have an advantage, the condition of being ahead and where we can afford to see this benefit for the good, like my neighbour! You know that fat ass bitch? Her crazy ass is about to get beaten the fuck up! The streets talk man, that shit that you have been running your mouth to, comes back to kick you in your own ass! This bitch has a code name, A.K.A Ghetto Bitch, just like her fat ass! Her husband went to prison for kicking her fat ass, well, her ass is big. Let me get back to what I was saying. Fat ass lets Ghetto Bitch's man drive her new car, you see Ghetto Bitch was not tripping on that because she drives it too! But when Fat ass saw Ghetto Bitch driving her car, she called the police and reported the car stolen but that is not the real problem to the situation.

Yeah, it's difficult to deal with or handle a problem child like Ghetto Bitch. Well, let me tell you, because I know your ass is nosey too, it's like this, when the cops pulled over fat ass' vehicle because it was reported stolen, fat ass thought that Ghetto Bitch would be driving the car. When the cops pulled over fat ass' vehicle, yeah, it was Ghetto Bitch's man who's driving it and now in jail facing a life sentence for driving a stolen car. Ghetto Bitch said, "You hoe! If my man does one more day in jail, you fat ass nasty hoe, I'm going to fuck you up and have my son kick your son's ass bitch!". Fat ass said "I'm not going to let him go to jail for my car, I love him!" Why in the hell did fat ass say that? Ghetto Bitch started beating the shit out of fat ass! Damn, Fat ass was beginning to get the best of Ghetto Bitch! Fat ass was on top of Ghetto Bitch and she pulled her bra off. Oh shit! Titties! This is the shit I'm talking about, a cat on a cat fight, this is the best fight that I have seen in a long time. Uh-oh! Ghetto Bitch is getting her come back, damn! A right hook to the chin! Can fat-ass shake it off? She's going down from the cheek to the jaw! That is one hell of a right hook by Ghetto bitch for the T.K.O. This is your sports announcer live in the projects, where you get it all Ladies and Gentlemen! As you see, a heavy weight against light weight. Fat ass weighing in at 300 lbs and the problem child better known as Ghetto Bitch light weight champion weighing in at 135 lbs and all ass! Let me tell you about them titties. Oh my God! It was edited from the T.V but only in the Ghetto you can show them titties without getting into trouble. If you missed it, the fight was a unanimous decision and still the champion by knock out is Ghetto Bitch! Well, I'm sitting here on the top of the staircase, laughing my ass off and realizing that ghetto life is not that bad at all to be true, it's what you make it. Like I said, everything could start to unravel. I allow myself a little downtime and closed my eyes. It had been a long and stressful week but the weekend promised to be off the hook and you can say it's interesting, the summer season of 1987.

I'm enjoying the crowds jamming in restaurants and the traffic tie-ups are so typical of a beach summer season. I'm in San Diego, you may wonder why I changed my mind so suddenly about the project life. I had seen the perfect candidate, surely it's not Gigi. It's been a year and a half since I had a woman as a friend. Well, a girlfriend, something like that. When you love someone for so long and you are sitting there waiting for them to love you back, your ass gets sore after a while and you get a big turnaround. They say I sounded grouchy when I answered that thought, well I know I'm not all sunshine, I have made some serious love investments that walked out on me. Hell! The one thing I miss about leaving the project are the bitches who just drop by anytime. If I may give you one bit of advice, mind to mind, but I do hope you'll rest for a while and don't start unpacking or trying to sort out your shit, certainly not tonight or tomorrow bitch because your ass is not living here! Are you sure you want to stay here? I don't think it's a good idea as suddenly as it began, just give me a moment and I'll be fine. I just feel a little out of breath, that's all. I want you to lean back and kick it, close your eyes because you can say you are dreaming because I'm not dying of heart failure so unexpectedly. No it is not a nightmare, this really happened! Well, are you ready? I'll draw up the papers. As you can see, I'm in San Diego getting my money and guess what my A.K.A is damn right if you say it T-MAC! I'll get my money and you won't have any more expenditures on it, would you? Well fuck you too, I like that name and out here in San Diego I'll put it in my application and I'll get the girls! You feel me! My best accommodation is the hoes sell their ass and gives me the cash. Bitch pussies come free but cracks cost money! Nasty mouth Guppie asking if she can suck my dick for a hit! Too many dicks have been in that mouth because for every money that you made tonight, somebody cummed and put AIDS in your mouth. I always like saying that to a hoe who asks if they can hit my weed or cigarettes, hell no bitch! Oh shit! Did I just tell on myself? I didn't just say weed huh? Well shit, I mean aren't you surprised, I intended to do it only once. I'm hungry so I open the refrigerator, a nigga got the munchies! I saw that it had been stocked, hell your ass got the munchies too, milk, Sunkist oranges, eggs, a big roast beef, a loaf of bread, some container of chicken soup and a small roasted chicken. I settle on making myself a roasted beef sandwich. I'm slicing a hot pickle, and Jalapeno cheese squeezer, mayonnaise, lettuce and tomato with onions, a little taste of heaven. My ass got comfortable in your refrigerator huh, you got me! I lied to you, I have been smoking weed for a long time, I'm a man now! That's why I don't have to say "Not me"! That thought and the image it conjured, ran through my mind, I'm a little absent- minded sometimes because of smoking some good weed, yeah man! and listening to some good entertaining music by Bob Marley! Getting Ivy on some evergreen leaves. I'm now a crack head but I know that a crack head would sacrifice their soul for a good hit of crack, to make you an offer because if they are your loved ones, you will be heartbroken. I had already made the same mistake several fucking times and I found myself wishing that Jeanette would say it again. But this time, Jeanette amended it with an additional "I don't want to know if shit is going down about them girls and my daughters. I have three girls in this house and we kick ass when it comes to other bitches so if you like our so called love, tell your little girlfriend's ass to start no shit and there will be no shit, okay young man!". I said "I don't have a girlfriend and I come out here to South East San Diego for one thing, to help my uncle Tank get that paper". I knew why Jeanette said that, because her daughters and my little brother, Light bulb and I are about the same age. Well, Tank has a son with Jeanette's older daughter Sharon, so it's only Kiana and April. My memory looking at Kiana is as beautiful and vivid as an evening star having intensely bright colors, full of vigor and freshness, expressive power and force. I can now see the images that were in my mind, is she real? She is an angel! My brotherly love continues, I don't forget to entertain strangers and by doing so, I unwittingly entertained an angel who is delightful and lovely, a girl who has preserved her youthful beauty. I know that light bulb has eyes for April, she is pretty. Out of the three, she looked more like her Mama Jeanette than all others. Sharon is the next in line to take her mother's beauty. Sharon is her second look alike, but all of them are so pretty. My lil' brother Light bulb and me The Mac, are living here in this house with them. I spend most of my time talking to Kiana, I was her friend and confidant as well as her family. She always call me to go with all her friends and she always keeps hooking me up with some of her girlfriends, but even though they were pretty, my heart belongs to her. I thought she looks like her Dad, well, she never talked about it so I never asked. She's a black red head with beautiful eyes and smile, she's light skinned than them all. April and Light bulb are somehow going together, he takes a place next to her on the love seat and is kissing her so passionately. They look like two love birds over there. My eyes turn to Kiana's lips, I realized that Kiana is the one who deserves my sympathy. I had not shared my feelings to her about the other people that she always hooks me up with because I am in love with her. Then Jeanette said, "T-Mac let me have a talk with you, in my room, okay!" I said, "All right, Jeanette!! As we are walking to her room, I keep on thinking what this is all about, "Now T-Mac!" Jeanette said "I can see that you like my baby Kiana, she's too young for you baby, give her one more year and she will be old enough for you T-Mac". But then, it seems that Jeanette have some hidden desires for me, she is in love with me! On the one hand, she loves me so much, on the other, she knew that I loved her daughter Kiana. Somehow, Jeanette's expression turned grief and I knew it but I said nothing! I just let her realize that thought all by herself. I wondered how her mind was dealing with the shock, since I'm not saying nothing to her she put her arm around me and said, "T-Mac did you hear me, T-Mac! I'm in love with you!" I looked her in the eyes then she smiled and said, "T-Mac you don't have to say you do too, but in time you will see I'm a good woman!"

The sound of the doorbell made us look up, it was Tank. So our conversation came to an end, Jeanette and Tank went to the hallway to talk by themselves. She is becoming more and more intent on showing her feelings about me but I have my heart set on Kiana. I can hear the tone of Jeanette's voice, and she sound all emotional but I could not make out what she was saying. Tank's back was against the wall with his hand on his forehead like he was thinking. I realized that she was crying, silent tears flowed down her cheeks and he puts his hand to her mouth to prevent her frustration and sobs. Tank looked like he has too much passion when he subject himself to her stress call. After being puzzled for a minute about was said in the hallways between them, I hurried out her bedroom not wanting her to see me thinking that she would be embarrassed if I see her so emotionally vulnerable, but she has already seen me standing there. I said, "If you need me, I can come back in ten minutes." Tank said, "No T-mac! You and I are going on a little ride Mac." In the car Tank said "But I can assure you that Jeanette will be all right today. Grego is at the spot at Dever Fever house, I need you to watch his back T-Mac, these niggas over here are ocean view 59 bims, you get to know them all. Grego knows the ones we fuck with, but when it comes to this dope game, no nigga can be trusted out here Mac. Oh, Mac! I'm going to get all of our cousins from La Salle because we need more soldiers, the spot is rolling! Jeanette loves your ass, Mac! What did you do to that woman for her to act like that?

I've known her for a long time and I have not seen her get that emotional for anybody, you must fuck the shit out of her last night Mac". I said, "No Tank, I like Kiana!", Tank said "Well Mac, you have to forget that shit! You have to take one for the team!" I said, "Huh?" Tank said, "I told Jeanette that I am going to get more of our cousins from L.A and she said no because she doesn't have a man and no man would like to be with her with all the niggas in her house, but if you will be her man, and they are your people, she knows that you will be cool with it and she will be too." I was thinking, I heard all this shit before, a feeling of loyalty and devotion to the team shit, Uncle Tank was looking more like Coach Leather when he said that shit! "Whassup! Grego" I said "Maccadosish is back!" Grego said, he always calls me that when he sees me. Grego said, "Maccadosish! I'm so glad you're here to help me roll the spot, I need a hustler like you Maccadosish", and Grego handed Tank I guessed that there are at least C-notes that slipped away from his hands to Tank hands, "O, Maccadosish!" Grego said, "Jeanette just called looking for you, I told her you're not here and she tells me I'm lying, brother!" Tank then shook his head and walked away. "I think you should call that woman and let her know that you are okay, the maccadosish is back!" Grego said with a big smile and said "You are making the women going crazy be careful, maccadosish!

Know what I'm saying? Jeanette is loco like a mofo but she is a good woman" I shrugged and pushed my chest out to play it off like there was nothing The Mac couldn't handle. I guess I have a fascination with danger because I see it all time in the projects, my family is the only ones who lives in the projects, there are no other related family who lives in the Ghetto but mine. "Hey T-Mac!" Dever Fever said "Ha...ha...ha T-Mac, you are having all these San Diego bitches going nuts over your sexy little handsome ass, if I were not pregnant, I will be all over you little ass Mac". Dever Fever is unseemly fair looking if she was not pregnant, she is pretty even with the condition of being pregnant though, she smiles with love and she has a pretty smile too.

People I come across thinks of me as being curt or having a brusque manner or the crack head mistake my shyness for unfriendliness, but it's my job to kick your ass when you come in our dope spot talking shit or thinking you can get over with something sick. I'm just the gunner in the spot and it doesn't bother me one way or another to put a bullet in your ass. I sat there nursing my big firearm, waiting on a fool to toss pennies in my wishing well, you know like Clint Eastwood said "Make my day punk and I will drive your ass to the dirt" It just reminds me of who I really was. "The phone is for you Mac", Dever Fever said. "Hello! T-mac if I did anything improper today", Jeanette said "I mean if I offended you I apologize, T-Mac okay?" I am not in a talking mood and Jeanette knows it too and she said, "T-mac come home tonight, I will cook a special dinner for you baby". I said "I will try Jeanette". "T- mac!" Jeanette said "I asked Tank if can you come home to eat and he said yes!" I made my way to her house, then she asked, "Are you going to tell me how you feel about me T-mac?", she sat next to me, her leg touching and warming mine under the table while I ate. "I was thinking, love can break your heart", I told her I have been in love to many times and got hurt all the time, then I changed the subject. I asked, "Are you eating?" "No T-Mac! I made this just for you baby", "Thank you Jeanette!" She smiled after I ate, although we were the kind of friends that kept it real with each other, she said "I'm sick and tired of being sick T-Mac", I said, "What's the problem?" "I'm lonely T-Mac!"

Her heartfelt words and cries caught my ass off guard, maybe the timing was not so good for us because this personal shit in my head was letting emotions settle in my mind, in place where I couldn't handle, "T-mac, women sometimes want to stop fucking and just to make love!" Everything had a label to her that said, "Not fucking but making love", you can find all the problems you want to know about a person over dinner. I then noticed a change of temperature in the dining room, from cold to hot! I don't allow any temporary excitement to distract us from the real business at hand, even with what I saw in her bathroom and bedroom, all her medicines bottles and all kinds of pills are almost gone and some are unopened, so I asked her all about the medicines bottles of pills with her name on them. "That's nothing" she said. I wiped the sweat away from my eyes, I am a young man and Jeanette is an older woman, "I think I had too much drink tonight, I can already see things in two" God! I just... I just... wanted to kiss her, she smiled a brief smile and I did too. For a moment we were two little kids and we kissed for a long time, we let the misty memories of our ex-lovers go in the heated passion that we had in each other's arms. I closed my eyes and had another thought of those bad memories that I had from time to time. I give a woman all my attention, but pain told me that in this life, real women start tripping when I quit dicking them down. My expression bothered her and the heat of the moment was suddenly gone, she said "What's your problem?" I didn't answer, I thought about it and shook my head. I know a man handles his own problems, she was the one I was worried about, it was always unspoken between us. As we made love all night, I left without telling her goodbye or that I loved her, like I was running away from any real love or emotions that burn inside me. We now understand our dysfunctional feelings for each other, it didn't seem like I had a choice at that time, I would have jumped and survived on the other side of the wall of Love, for Kiana! I told myself that I'd made some fucked-up choices in my life, well that Ghetto money and food stamps are calling me! This Uncle Tom is a nigga in the spot running game on us, Grego! "I don't wanna lose my fuckin' woman, man I got three kids, they watch that TV brother! I will look out when I get some money, this is all I got, Grego!" The crack head said. Damn! I can still remember how he looked up at us, that nigga could win an Oscar award, I looked back towards Grego then he smiled and said, "Look brother, I will give you one more week to have my money". "Okay Grego! I'll have it, I promise! I will man, can I get a hit!" Grego looked puzzled for a minute with a mistrust look on his face, I wanted to give his ass a haymaker's uppercut to the chin, Grego said, "You are a good man Arto, I'm going to give it to you." Grego felt sorry for this nigga, I said "Hold on! Arto nigga, you have one week only or I will put one in your ass", I showed him my gun, and he kept going like the energizer bunny, it made me want to kick the shit out of Arto's ass, something made me ease the thought in my mind.

A few seconds later, a crack head drunk was in front of me, talking how bad he's hurting but in a drunken voice, that shit was funny as hell. Grego said "Tangle what's going on my brother?" He was bleeding like a stab of pain hit him, he was hurting pretty bad. Grego took a step forward to him and said, "Tangle who beat you up?" Tangle said, "The niggas down the street tried to take my money Grego, those niggas hate you so watch your back man!" From that day on, I liked Tangle, he is a soldier, he keeps his money even when someone kicks his ass and he was drunk and out. I like this brother, the drugs didn't make him soft like most crack head, they would have given up their money or take a small piece of dope for their money, and the pusher get over on them, I told Grego I'll be back and he said, "Where are you going Maccadosish?" I said, "Down the street to see who those niggas are Grego!" "Wait a minute!" Grego said, "Maccadosish, those niggas are down the street, they are not in front of the house short stopping customers brother, I don't give a damn what those niggas do down the street, that's on them, as long as it is not out in front of our shit Maccadosish baby." "Grego!" I said, "I hear what you are saying love one but I have to see who are these niggas who are hating us, we are blind men walking in to a bullet, Grego! My pop's always told me, it's a helluva to be surprised and disappointed, and believe me Grego it's not going to be a damn disappointment on our end okay!"

This was the picture-perfect life we all wanted, I glanced around and I saw the niggas on the street corner, I got invited into their playground, I had to unplug them gangster niggas. I mean, see where there heart at. I put on my game face, I looked well dressed in all black.

I looked at all three of them, they stood there like frozen chickens, I gave them a look that said, "Nigga! You don't grab a man money in the ghetto without expecting a fight mofucker". I sat down on the corner curb across the street from them, they could see the gun handle sticking out my wrist band, my eyes glazed over at them, their souls were like sinking in a quicksand. The niggas went to the staircase without looking back, I stood up and went to the spot, I'm not trying to draw attention to myself but these niggas got to know that a brother is not playing in this dope game. "What's up love ones!" They are mostly my cousins from South Central California, L.A h1 boys La Salle Hustler! Man, it was a full house! There was Q-loc, Pat, Dog-ski, my older Brother Silk-E, Big-E, Lucky, L.J, Todd, Nestle Crunch, Pooh, Charlie and Tray. We were making money and smoking weed nonstop for the last thirty-five hours.

Dever Fever said, "Are you guys staying here for a couple of days?" All of us said no. Q-Loc said, "Dever Fever you have a lot of kids now!" She smiled, got up and walked around the living room paced in her house robe, the cornbread and buttermilk walk taking her gifts from above, with a big smile on her face, and her arms folded under her modest and big firm breasts, laughter stiffening her tongue, she is pushing out her top lip, I watched her. Dever Fever saw me staring at her, then she came and sat by my side, kissed my cheek and touched my hand, she said something but with all the buzz of conversations in the living room, I couldn't hear her, then she paused until I was looking at her, my eyes studied the seriousness in her eyes, she didn't blink, I stood and said, "Dever Fever, it's going to be alright, believe me sweetheart, no nigga's going to fuck with you because we got your back Dever Fever", she said "Cool! It's like I'm one of the boys or something?" We laughed then she said, "I was catching feeling, dammit! All y'all dicks in my house, that shit made me tingle but my ass is pregnant. It made her eyes look tight, we looked at each other and she licked her lips, I said "Don't do that. Lick your lips like that!" She touched her breasts, ran her fingertips around her nipples, she moved her breasts over my chest, rubbed her sexy face against mine, and said. "You cannot handle this T-mac." I said. "Don't put on a show for me Dever Fever, just do it!" She stood up and motioned for me to come to her bedroom with her, we were in her room, she closed the door and the she kissed me, it was our first time kissing, she shivered and whispered, "O, my God!" I said "What?" She said. "I have been wanting to kiss you T-mac, you are so good baby!" Her legs opened and trembled. She was making me come, I was on my feet, she reached back and held my dick in her hands, she had very soft hands, moved it slowly and fast up and down, man! She has magic hands, no one had ever made me come in their hand like that before, she is good, damn I love this shit! I rubbed my fingers between her legs, massaged that big pussy nice and slow, someday! Some-fucking-day this is mine, with a big smile on my face.

I grabbed a chair and pulled it up to the living room window thinking about my crazy life and what just happened is the far craziest shit I have ever done. I stared out at the crack heads' community that had been destroyed by people like me, the black man just had to be the trash man, It made me say to myself, "Yeah, me too, the poorest trash man, singing that I'm going to come" Well, crime had paid and paid really well. I sat my attention back to hustling, to work the spot we always were busily and quickly, slang to make money by unquestionable means, and we got that paper man, who can you fuck with a team of killers who grow up together from the sand box, real relatives Kinfolk, a big ass player family reunion, no dumb ass would get in the way of this household, he would be a damn fool! When you find out we are all folks, his ass will be fucked up, rib cages kicked, kicked in the gut. He wheezed with each blow after blow, but Grego will always save their lives, women after women coming to the spot of sucking dicks. Dever Fever looked at me with jealous eyes but didn't say anything, that call left me in the fucked up situation. Jeanette said, "Someone told me you are a fucking ugly pregnant bitch Dever Fever, I and the girls will be coming down there to stomp that baby out that nasty hoe, I'm going to fuck both of you up." I told Dever Fever the first right to refusal because of the fact that we were fucking around, before Jeanette and her daughters come from down the streets kicking in the door. I went down the street to meet her before she comes to the spot acting like a fool, the dope spot is already on fire and we don't need more attention here than it's all ready have.

Jeanette has been supportive and vulnerable, I knew I can sweet talk her back in love for a moment. I saw that killer look in her eyes, you know, the look that your woman gets when she wants to know who else was sucking your dick. "Are you crazy, Jeanette?" She took her hardware out so I said, "Put that gun up baby." I gave her a sexy smile and kissed her, told her I loved her for the first time then she cried! Tears of joy, and said, "I think you just got lucky T-Mac" then she made a face and handed me her gun after a good night of perfection. It is a beautiful thing when shit comes out right in the end, when I was lying from the beginning, being an aggressive youth overwhelms her with that Mac Love. Give away a little more until the next time it comes out and she is all mine, that's right player! Women are shit! You have to play the game and work your ass. Like Jeanette, all she wanted to be is like Queen Bee, hell! all brothers want to be a King! Sshh! I didn't say shit, okay? I remembered how she kissed me, her tongue all the way down my mouth, standing on tiptoes and she said, "T-mac, I'm not trying to play a game or trap you, I love you Baby!" My hand moved between her legs, massaged her fat ass pussy through her jeans, her legs opened and she told me to stop but she let my hand slide inside her jeans. My fingers went to work inside her, she was wet, and her heat was rising like she was climbing something. I was getting hard, she moved her body slowly against my finger inside her, the stops turned into "Yes baby right there!" And a sweet song came in my head. She liked the way I moved my finger, "Oh...Oh...Oh...!" Her mouth was shaped like the letter O, "O yes right there!" She was all smiles and giggles and restless! Butterfinger licking good! "Hey lady, I will make you melt in your panties, oh, you're the good wife now". Hell, you see all the shit a brother has to do to keep a sister happy with a gun in her hands. Let's be real, it took all I had to know to backhand her ass down that street, she owed me for the damage she did to me. I'm good huh to be able to turn that shit around, to make her feel bad for being right. I told you that, I will be an international player, well, a so called player! After that shill all went down, Dever Fever was cool with me, she started fucking with people like a real player would say, keep it in the family right? Key of dope after key of dope, we were getting off and all the thugs and hustlers in San Diego loved us, and those who fucked with us, you damn sure come up!

For the remainder of the day, the house was not entirely empty, thanks to O'clock appointments or you can call it, buttcall! It was Q-Loc, me, and the door man, Stephon who is a big ass nigga! I mean big! Well he's family too because he is my girl Jeanette's brother, but Stephon was a cool brother. What happens in the spot stays in the spot before Stephon would tell his sister. Hell just froze over, and I don't really mind saying that he really frightened niggas, hell we were all frightened mofucker, nigga didn't know how to come at a player in this family. I call us the blue-bloods from hell! I mean, some of my family are crips and some are bloods, all under the same roof! How can you fuck with niggas who are from opposite games that normally kill each other off, a mofucker have to think twice.

The room looked ghetto - fabious, on the table we had a silver platter full of weed, and we had whiskey, hand rolled cigars full of weed and Hennessy, Q-Loc and I are in the spot making that money. We were getting low on the chronic weed so we called out our chronic connection, his name is Chino! A sureno, from El Monte-Flores S.G.V, in San Diego getting his paper too. "Whassup, Chino!" I said. "T-mac! Q-Loc, what's going down homie?" I have some bum ass shit player and Q-Loc was coughing the whole time he was talking to Chino I said, "Hell homie! What's your price for two pounds of this bum?" "T-Mac, for you guys, I will give it for three thousand a pound." Then we have an understanding. "Big pimpin!" I said, "We can do some good business Chino!" and Chino said, "Sure business homie, nothing personal, just business." Q-Loc said, "Right!

We have a lot of money, Chino player is getting payed," Chino said "As long as your pay check is all good in your end, there's no problem on this end," Q-Loc and I made chronic smoke dance in our throats. When you have money, everyone serves you, we lit up another one, I took two puffs but I hate the smoke, the smell brings back memories, good and bad. I was sipping my drink of Hennessy in apple juice then I recognize the reflection of myself in High school when the thugs in the restroom were smoking weed and the cops said, "In prison or get killed!" So fucking beautiful, as beautiful as the young man I'm trying to forget. My eyes turned sensitive, these memories softened my conniving heart and pain, hummed along with the classical music Q-Loc was playing on the turn table, scratching and rapping. We are always rapping in the spot, yes, maybe one day Q-Loc is going to be a big rap star! Hell his ass can spit some lyrics, he will give you a rush from wall to wall of rap, like running water in a peaceful river, every slow rap is wetter than the one before.

The thick weed smoke lingered over the living room like smog over long beach, the smoke irritated my eyes so I opened the window closer to the front door. It was darker in our spot than it was outside so I turned on every light switch I can find in the house. We always have a little fuck-up-our spot party, I could see leftover cans of beer and cigarette butts everywhere, the room had been destroyed.

My heart was in a dark place right now, plus I'd never been good with women, not when I had to play the boyfriend and read between the long fuck up emotion lines like that place called Jeanette where most of her emotions are alive. I felt more than lust, much more than that, love can handicap a woman's heart like a handicapped prisoner. She asked me when can she see me again and that surprised me so I said, "Do you want to see me tonight Jeanette?" "Yes, baby!",she said "But Jeanette, there's no one here with Q-Loc and your brother Stephon and I got some things to take care of." "T-Mac, you can call me anytime, even if you can't come through, ring my phone and let me know you're okay in that dope spot baby! Why can't you leave for a while T-Mac?" "No Jeanette, I told you baby, Q-loc will be by himself and I'm going to help him clock in a few dollars." Everything seemed normal, too normal that it was not like Jeanette, it was like I was talking to her impersonator, or I'm actually the king! That shit surprised me too, I peeped towards the front to see who had pulled up since I was on the place feeling like a king, and I guess Jeanette knows she is Queen Bee. Hell, all the girls in Southeast San Diego knows Jeanette and for me to get a permit, the women have to consent to me that they don't know her before I express my hand like a cop on your ass about a license to drive a car. Girls have authority fucking with me because Jeanette made it known that I'm a property that belongs to her ass, sounds right! Believe me downright! Perhaps she thinks she has this side of the hood lock down, it may be, but I'm still The mac. With all this shit I'm dealing with, I did the best I could. Damn it! I held my breath, I expected it to the game, to need a password, there was no ring on her finger, cold air came in through the broken rear window. Hold on, I have to pull that king screen back up, damn pop-ups! I'll have to go out and surface to the upper one outside, it was Jeanette, Kiana and bog-Ski, if I'm looking at this right. You should be able to see that my love for Kiana make my inside jump, right now all three of them look like suspects. Stephon said, "T-mac her comes my sister and she looks mad as hell mac," It was not like I was deep inside with my new lover or something to challenge my brain, crazy was the answer. That had been bugging me, something else was tugging at the back of my mind and Jeanette walked like, "I'm gonna fuck up some bitches in this house", one foot directly in front of the other, she turned on the look to kill as she got in front of the door. An ungodly midget who was ten feet tall, Jeanette said, "I will make them glitch bitches move out the city," Stephon said, "Hold on Jeanette, come on in sis! There's no one here but me, T-mac and Q-loc, funny you asked about them glitches, you got me curious who you are talking about, me or T-Mac?" She was on the edge of a roundabout as per the look on her face, like saying all shit and couldn't care less look. She's all about getting her way looking around the spot then she said, "Keep it that way!" I told her, but she didn't trust me. She could get the goods, but only got the good weed smoke in the wind.

She had access to other things like how much weed I'm fucking with, she had to make sure that her man didn't get fucked over or got some good new pussy. There's no honour among players, never has been, never will be.

Dog-ski said, "Whassup Q-Loco, Mac Baby! You know what's down that way?", he said that looking at Jeanette, he gave me a look telling me not to worry about shit and said, "You feel me Mac baby!" And we laughed the he said, "I can smell it!

Fire it up," Q-Loc handed him a two finger extended look like a fat ass cigar full of chronic high in the mofucker. Then Jeanette talked to Stephon, looking at me fucking off my high. "Jeanette, if I may say, I'm glad to see that you look a bit more rested, today was a very difficult day for everyone who love Jeanette," she said, "Are you forgetting something T-Mac?" with a smile, but in an odd and certainly unexpected way, being here in Jeanette's world is giving her the love she is giving to me. I feel almost as though I've lived here with her all these years, I kissed her smiling lips, the expression on Jeanette's face was just as happy but I still couldn't let her inside my heart and I was the loser because my heart still beats for Gigi. I run a never ending race of love for her.

Gigi's heart is dead and turned away from me. Why Gigi? And even though you had only made it right from the start, I don't want to cry anymore, my experience with her changed the appearance of my heart for the better, I was loyal to you! My heard raced to the finish line, but you passed it up! Why Gigi. why? If you didn't plan on being in my life, you shouldn't have started loving me because I was doing just fine by myself, being stress free T-Mac.

Jeanette said, "I was thinking my heart went to its last grave, and my feelings all died," That was it! Gigi felt the same way about me. I said to Jeanette, "I couldn't, with any conscience handle a transaction like love, and I beg you not to waste your love on me," The subject changed and it looked pretty good, but then she said, "No T-Mac," she just cuts me off, "T-Mac, let me speak to you in the back room," She knew the light was red but there's no question about it, she was going through a greenlight wish, I know because my heart has been there before, and to top it off, I told her the love is not there anymore. She was thinking that we are going to retire in some beautiful community somewhere, "T-Mac!" Jeanette said, "It's my responsibility to tell you baby!" I was thinking she fucked someone other than me because I'm down here at the spot all the time, and she doesn't get some dick all the time. Hell, because she always have some big T-shirt on! It's been a year since we've been together and I have not seen her titties, or suck them, not one time! She always talks about us making love, hell, can I make love to them titties? "T- Mac, I'm dying baby, I have breast cancer. I know you always think I'm not sexy in bed all the time having some T-shirt on, but I don't want you to see that I only have one breast, the doctor cut off my breast, or it will spread all over my body T-Mac. I have to start my chemotherapy." Why not just withdraw and make it all disappear, I keep saying to myself when she cries in my arms, all my life I was thinking that a lover of mine will die of old age or get killed, but to love someone that is dying, and there's nothing you can do to help them and no one can. I hold her, my heart went bitter for the first time in my life. I had nothing to say or think about but her. "Jeanette, I'm here. Just remember that if you want to talk to someone, can I help you with anything?" "Yes T-Mac! Don't tell my kids I'm dying and be here for me T-Mac. You make me happy baby, you make the pain go away, I've never been so happy with someone like you T-Mac. Besides, I don't have enough picking up after my husband, how much can a woman love a man? Sweetheart, be happy for me because I'm happy I have you!" She had penetrating brown eyes that bespoke intelligence and she had a smile that inspired confidence. And in fact, that confidence is well placed for, as her associates and we know, she missed very little about her dying wishes. She called me by my real name for the first time, she made me make a promise to her, to always look for her daughters. She smiled at the memory, but her smile faded as she realized that I had tears in my eyes. I felt that one day, I might see my ex-lover Gigi and we can still be friends, but Jeanette will always be in my memory, looking up to the kingdom of heaven at hand.

Heal the sick, cleanse the lepers, raise the dead, I'm crying out and praying for God to have mercy on Jeanette's soul. Somehow, Jeanette and I live life like we did not have that conversation that day, but it was never too easy. Jeanette let me look at her breast, stepping back but still holding my arms with both hands. Though afraid, she would not like to see the look on my face, and in all honesty I guess I did pretty well, I've got some excellent clients. I open my mouth and put one of her breasts in, then I suck it so good. There was a world of understanding in Jeanette voice, I said, "You're just as pretty as I knew you'd be Jeanette". "Oh yes, I'm fine, it's just... well, you see T-Mac I'm going to make you a real ladies' man, women will not be able to handle you T-Mac! Baby, I'm going to give you a name about women's scandal that a bitch brings about playing bitch games on men, so when you fall in love again, yes baby! Will you stop looking at me so crazy like and just hear what I'm saying to you?" She was right about the scholarly look and my characteristics as a player, but who can give you a game more than a woman? Brother believe me, no one!

I pulled a chair from a nearby table and sat down, she teaches me anthropology and about the behaviour of man. She is standing over me, I'm looking up at her thinking why she was saying all this, and it come to me, she will always be there for me, her wonderful thoughtful love, and she will always be with me in mind and soul! She bent down to kiss me, my cousin Charlie thought I was in hot water, Charlie said, "You've got to let us have an after dinner drink with y'all and Jeanette you can cook your ass off," Jeanette gave him a look, like saying, "You see, I'm talking to my man?" And Charlie knew it too, he said, "You don't have to worry about me Jeanette, I'm harmless", and Charlie ran out on me. I can see the back room from where I was sitting, Big-E and Lucky was blowing one big fat ass blonde, I can hear Q-Loc's voice saying the famous quote he always says after a meal "Nothing like some good smoke after a meal!" passing an OL'english around blowing chronic smoke in the 8 ball bottle. Something bothered April today, something Light bulb had noticed subconsciously. It registered mentally but had not made an impression at the moment, what could it have been? April said, "Light bulb, are you fucking that Katlin Bitch huh?" Light bulb said, "You are not fucking me!" And April started crying, ran to her room, and slammed the door. Sharon hooked up my older brother Silk-E with one of her friend, Michelle, and Michelle has a cousin who was not scared of Jeanette and that girl loves the shit out of me. One day she told me to come over to her house, she sneaked me in her room, immediately slipped off her clothes and said, "T-Mac, fuck me in my ass," I immediately took off my shirt, jumped on top of her on the bed, her legs were open, she had a sexy looking pussy. I quickly hold my dick in my hand before she changed her mind. I was sticking my dick in her pussy and I was happy for some fly-by-night pussy, oh yes! But hell, she started saying "No T-Mac! No! Not there, put it in my ass!" I had a questioning face, because this is going to be the first girl I will ever fuck in the ass, "That's right," she said simply. "The ass T-Mac, fuck me in the ass Mac!" We tossed about in the bed, she found that she could take no satisfaction in having me fuck the shit out of her sexy pussy. I was enjoying the thought of me opening up her back door, if it makes her feel any better, I'm going to fuck the shit out of her ass, and I mean ass too!

The freak was an attractive young woman with dark sexy eyes and olive skin. It is lovely, isn't it?' But then I really don't know much at all about any ass fucking, do I? I could not help feeling uncomfortable, I waited for the invitation to enter her back door, she would not have a bitter disappointment, I stepped back, closing my eyes on that tight butt hole. My dick greeted that ass, it was really very close to going inside, I was smiling while reminiscing. I think she was having a great deal of difficulty with my dick going up her ass, but as she said, "Fuck it mac, it's yours Mac! Fuck me baby!" All the shit feels so damn good! The only loud sound was her, well, me too saying, all shit baby! But it was nearly four o'clock in the morning, there was someone checking the door lock, I'm careful about locking up, she said, "Yes, hold on a minute grandmother! She was whistling in my ear, "Go in the closet Mac," she opened the room door then her grandma said, "You have a boy in my house girl?" "No! Grandma," "You are lying girl! I heard you two in here. Boy, are you under the bed?" I was afraid that the old lady was going to find me butt naked in the closet sitting on the big piles of shoes. The closet door opened fast, the old lady looked down at me and said, "I'm going to go get my .357 magnum," I made up my mind to get the hell out of this crazy ass lady's house, do you blame me for being nervous of an old lady? Hell, I was not going to stick around to see if she can see or not, she can be a marksman, you feel me?

It was Ld, Todd and Nestle Crunch, it's funny how Nestle Crunch got his nick name. One day, he shaved his head bald and on the back of his head were razor bombs, well you know black ass nigga, back of his head looked like a Nestle crunch bar. Well they were at the spot with Grego, I can hear them in the house talking shit to each other about who among the new bitches is the ugliest. My ass is on the side of the house smelling like ass, butt naked, thinking about that freak bitch who owes me a new pair of silk boxers. I run off and left it on her bedroom floor and I don't mind saying that it was worth it, as a matter of fact I loved it.

I was destined to wander forever like a lover of broken dreams, passionately proud that he was the great-great lover. I can smell the weed smoke coming out the window over the sink framed by the beautiful oak tree that stood at the side of the house where I'm standing while putting on my clothes. Well, I guess I should say welcome to the real ghetto, feeling clearheaded and refreshed for the first time in several days. It was Jeanette calling, almost apologetically, she began "T-Mac, I love you baby and thank you for yesterday. It meant so much to me and please baby don't agree to this unless it's something you really want to do." I knew that Jeanette could have no more kids, and by us adopting Myesha, she would have a child to raise as our own and I will enjoy it very much. "Jeanette," I said "Myesha, Kiana, and April were getting along fine, they love the thought of having a stepsister. Well, Sharon on the other hand, it's hard knowing what's on her mind, she reminds me of her mother who is my Girl Jeanette.

Friday night. Jeanette and I are dressing up in some fly ass clothes plus she had agreed to have dinner with me this Friday night. Whenever she and I go out for dinner to sea port village, I always chose fairly priced restaurants. People always tell us what a great couple we were, Jeanette also liked the fact that she wore only mascara and almost natural lipstick, she always has a sophisticated way to supply make up on her face. It was clear that she was used to the best, the restaurant was animated by all kinds of women and men, Jeanette said, "I'm so glad we came here baby", I knew what she meant, "Yes, of course Jeanette, I'll be at the bar!" Jeanette took in the hum of conversation, the animated face of the well-dressed senior citizens at the bar with me. Jeanette asked me, "Baby, are you all right?" I said, "Don't worry about me, I'm okay." In my mind, I was thinking that this place is too rich for my blood, but that reminds me. The truth is, I hate cocktail parties where the only person I know is my supposed to be date, and she is running mouth, well she reasoned that it was a large gathering of people, surely I could find someone to talk to. She remembered me sitting by myself at the end of the bar, she had a way of doing something, a movement or a way of generally requiring skill and dexterity.

The conversation I had, was with an older but still sexy woman sitting at the bar with me, she reminds me of Mary. Oh, for the love of God, it's hard forgetting Mary. We both returned to enthusiastically greeting one another, I looked embarrassed or the old hurt hit my heart that she has a sexy body. Her breasts are beautiful, that stick out of that dress she has on, she said, "I'm sorry I'm not good at remembering names, and I was trying to place you." I felt isolated in this situation, could this be Mary? No! I'm tripping Mac I said to myself, too bad though because most of them aren't nearly as attractive as her. She waited while I continued to look at her, her eyes were more green than blue, her long blond hair attractively flecked with grey, with a raised eyebrow she asked me, "Will I pass inspection?" And she's good because I looked puzzled, can't I see she's trying to make something out of this and it's nothing. For the love of heaven, she looks like an older version of Mary, I stared now at her sexy figure with lively eyes and soft honey- blond hair. I could see the fine Hennessy that detracted not a bit from Mary's lovely tan complexion and as she stared, the memories of Mary flooded my heart.

Damn! Jeanette came who always makes her a part of our conversation or arguments and protesting in our conversations thinking that she knew me. Jeanette brought about the downfall of good memories of my past, the lady got up and walked away then Jeanette smiled and said, "I got a good memory, I love to sculpt the character of that bitch hawking my man. I have a photographic memory, that bitch last week was staring at you, and today it's more practical, she want my man! And in all honesty baby, I guess I'm pretty good. I've got some excellent client.

Hell, Jeanette had just been selected for the player hater award, she has her master making a good living now as a photographer of pretty good memories. It's a shock, I guess I may never get over anyway, it's still hard to talk about Mary, why do things like this has to happen? Then Jeanette's tone brightened, "Baby, shall we order our food?" she said. Over dinner we caught up on our ex-lovers, where she met her ex-husband, someone she actually dated when she was still a teenager and married him, "My second and last husband," she said, "is absolutely wonderful, T-mac. He died years ago, and do I ever miss him! We weren't one of the wealthy people, but we had a sweet house in a wonderful section of Coronado, he had an adequate income," but Jeanette saw a brief flicker of uncertainly crossed her face and realized in that moment that she didn't love that man without the smile or cheerful expression, she always has a little more paint about the last one, but it was really all right.

When we see that our life is at a red light and seems to be at an end, only you and I know where we are at the time life take us through. Fully done or finished completely, painstakingly accurate or careful, telling ourselves, "This cannot be, what's happening to me?" When we are there, we are at a red light, damn that traffic light!" A diverting or edifying narrative of real or imaginary events for the total: the earthquakes tale of thousands of pains in our life kills the woes! The natural endowment or ability of a superior quality, this is the new me look, hay I'm cool with it thoughts, but deep down, you gifted people collectively, that the company which makes good use of talents, old love or money pains in our lives. Having an inclination to talk about the intersection of our life accidents, a tale with a tease peepshow in our life, we all do them huh, think about it. Tell us our stories, you know, the shit! The sexiest new show on the planet! Out with the old, and in with the new beginning. The shit we have in our minds, dancing up in the star, stars with the stripes, the hottest dancers in this spectacular world premieres us! I know it dusts me, everything is hotter in the heart, the things we don't want to go through, we will end up at indoor-outdoor cultural of love's relation to pain!

The cultural anthropology, the scientific study of human culture based on archaeological ethnologic, social and psychological data and method of analysis that compares our life. Can you tell me something different under the sun? When a player over bets the river of life, it usually means one of two things; he's bluffing because he missed his hand - a busted flush or a straight draw, or he has a strong hand and is trying to make it look like he loves bluffing and you put a lot of pressure on your love opponent, they want to call you because they want to win that big pot, they want to take a shot of this love game again, they are thinking it's 50-50 and that I'm not bluffing, so when they see or think it's love their heart always over bets in the big pot, they want to take a shot at it K-Q or two pairs the King and Queen and moves all in together, then I'd be kind of committed to his so-called love game, and now I'd have to play this big pot with just a pair of old hurts, having a flush draw. You choose to play it a little bit safer this time, but to disguise my hand, to modify the manner or appearance of order to Yes and No's to prevent recognition, to conceal or obscure by dissemblance or false show; misrepresent - disguise one's interest, some time to disgrace because of loss of honour, respect or reputation. We say we live up to no shame, but we feel that we do, having the synonyms: disgrace, dishonor, shame, infamy, ignominy, odium, scandal, obloquy, opprobrium, disrepute, discredit, degradation, to disgraceful, bringing and mindful of warranting disgrace! And damn, those are disagreeable moods, now you are telling me you have not been there? You are not human, I can't talk about you, and that's the shit, I'm talking about! You feel me? Only a driver and a passenger know the feeling of breaking down on the side of the road, the life has a long road ahead of us, reality sets back in and we move on! The big happy green light always puts back on smiling faces.

She had skills, when I told Jeanette that I was about to come, she took all of me in her mouth, made sexy greedy sounds and swallowed all I had to give, she kept going until I was drained and became too sensitive in her mouth. I had to hold her face and ask her to stop, she bathed my dick with her tongue before she moved away. She rested her head in my lap and she looked up, her smile was wide but hot, it turns me on to be honest, I miss being with... with a black woman, I had no idea I needed her. I need her back stories, her pains, I need her to give me all that, and let me give her all mine, before SDPD caught me speeding and running a red light down the road of love. On the way home, I hit that strip between love and hate and opened the bitches up, by the time we zoomed and passed by Zzyzx exit sign of love, we find out that we were moving like a jet plane. I reached over, rubbed her one breast, I bet that made her panties wet, I sure did have a big orgasm when she had me in her mouth. She was having multiple orgasms, I treated her like she was a candy.

We think that is inevitable, all people expect that at some point in life, they are beautiful and rich, we all expect men to be men. Jeanette's eyes darkened because those are the eyes of a woman scorned, men hurt them. I shook my head, I don't like being fucked over, not at all. Want a confession? I told myself that there's no way for that to happen again, to laugh an angry laugh and intense laugh, the bitter kind of love that showed the dark side of a person's soul. We found out all we could about life, fast love is sometimes not what it says it is, you know the slang! Like a drug addiction, have a monkey on one's back, a person who is mocked, duped, or made to appear a fool for love, "monkey see, monkey do" for real! It makes you want to tie that monkey game to the tree, to expect to be purchased with the major one, "I love you"

The relationship that Dever Fever and Pooh had is over, all of us at the spot are having a meeting, "Tank let us know if that shit is looking good, money man! Get your money man!" We all blow some chronic, we have some new player at the spot, Michael, who is Jeanette's other brother and we have Freddy white shoe. Let me tell you, why we call Freddy, the white shoe, this nigga is a leprechaun always shining his white shoes with a toothbrush and toothpaste, Freddy white shoe had the whitest shoes I have ever seen in my life, and those shoes are not new, it was about five years old. I remember I had a pair when they come out in 82ᵗʰ, he makes his shoes glossy and so bright, he polishes them three to five times a day, yes, you know that nigga became the shoe shine boy. Hell, all of us had our shoes off for his ass to hook them up and immediately my feet and ankle bones receive strength, at the same time refreshing, fresh and clean. This nigga named Eddy has gold and his neckline was dressed in gold, this nigga looked like, Mr. T on the A Team. The first time I saw Eddy in the spot, he had two big guns in his waist band and a fine champagne cognac in his hand Remy Martin. I said, "This nigga looks cool in a mofucker," to myself. I promised to myself that I wouldn't diss niggas who are on the grind with us, oh, I almost forgot (how dare I) this nigga Eddy-B is not a killer, why in the hell does he have two guns but is not going to kill shit. One day, Silk-E and Light Bulb, Q-Loc and me were at the spot, Eddy-B ran to the spot crying and shit about some Mexicans who jacked him for all his gold, so Silk-E, Light Bulb, Eddy-B, and myself jumped in my four door Cadillac, Jeanette gave the car a name, Dollar! And dollar is a hoe-catcher with lime green paint, and avocado color leather top, the interior is avocado color suede, dark limo tint window, sitting on Laces on 13's, two foam's antennas, one phone L.A. area code 213, the other S.D. area code 619, we will be on 805 Highway. When we get to the 5 Freeway San Diego, phone will cut off, we called the L.A. phone, the orange 76 Ball, because we had one on the L.A Foam antenna, so when you see Dollar coming your way, and we are looking for your ass because you fucked us out of some money, if your mind is like 100 cents, your ass knows that you should run.

We get up to the shopping centre where Eddy-B said the mexicans jacked him at, Eddy was looking for them, I was driving around slowly in the parking lot, Eddy said, "There he go!" I was looking all around for a big ass Mexican gangster, man I know this nigga is not talking about this little ass person, "Eddy!" Silk-E said, "Are you sure he's one of them Eddy?" "Yes, Silk-E he's the only one who jacked me!". I knew this nigga got to be kidding, "Eddy!" I said "Does he have a gun man?" "No!" Eddy said. I looked at Eddy like, "You are a bitch!" the paisa looked like Mr. T. Paisa got all of Eddy's gold shit on, that shit was funny, Silk-E and light Bulb jumped out the Cadillac doors while Eddy was still sitting in the front passengers seat. I said to Eddy "Go help, my brothers got your shit back nigga!" Eddy had a scared to die look on his face, I gave him a look saying "Nigga, I will fuck your bitch ass up too!" He got out of the car then I went to find a parking space. I saw Silk-E gave an uppercut to the paisa, hit him in the rib cage and Light Bulb kicking him in the gut, the little paisa took off running. Silk-E and Light Bulb are now in the street on the corner of the shopping center, hell, this is an all Mexican neighbourhood and you know the deal, some of them decided to help paisa's ass. This big ass Sureno took a haymaker to Silk- E's Chin, damn it should feel like shit, Silk-E just shake it off.

Light Bulb is still in paisa's ass, more Mexicans come to help, I ran over there to help my brothers kick some Mexicans ass or get our black asses kicked, it was going down, there are about six Mexicans and only three blacks fighting our asses off, Silk-E displays blow after blow and stumble the Sureno.

I was chasing one Mexican around a parked car in the street, Light Bulb had the paisa on the ground making him take off the gold that belongs to Eddy, damn! Silk-E just kicked out the Sureno in the middle of the street, when the other Mexicans saw that shit, all of them ran down the street. I guess to say, every man for themselves. Hell, you're right, all this time I'm describing this tragic fight between different races and not one bothered to stop to help, where's the unity at? And we got the nerve to say, "One Love!" Oh, I almost forgot, I called Eddy a bitch, yeah! I did. Where is his ass at all this time we were fighting for this his shit? Well if your ass is dumb, you would not know, that nigga ran off on us, "Shhh, hey you Eddy-B! You are a Bitccchhh…!", And Arto couldn't pay the debt he owe us and Grego sued Arto crack head's ass, Grego said, "Look Arto man, my people wants to kick your ass for that money you owe us, you know indebted for about C-note Arto, if you cannot pay it off, you have to clean up the house, and make the store run Arto, and if you ran off with the money Arto, I don't want to hear no shit!" "I'll pay it back!" "Oh yes, you will out your ass when all my folks stomp the shit out of you Arto!"

Man, Arto was a crack head behind all the score cards, he knew we will come after him. Tan said, "We all don't need to be in the spot at the same time, if the cops kick down the front door and find some crack in the spot, all of you will be going to jail, so we are going to work two shifts. Now, pick a person you like to work with on your shifts." So Q-Loc and I picked each other to work in the spot at daytime. I knew Jeanette would love that shit, I'm coming home every night to sexy mama. She had a clear bright smile when I told her that I will be home at night and she will sing me a good night lullaby to sleep every night. Man, I can see that shit in my head, well I asked Jah for a woman who will love me with all her heart and I can say it, it's Jeanette! For real! Believe me, okay, I need to come stronger than that. I was just saying! I can't handle myself, I unclenched my jaw, to say hi to her, took a breath, slow and deep.

"What's a girl like you so beautiful, doing in a place like this? You don't look like the type of a sexy woman who'd be hanging out in a flea market," she nodded and said, "Guess I have a big fascination for silk panties in a blue-jeans world." She ran her hand over her long curly hair that went down to her sexy hour glass body, her eyes were green that said deep love when you look into them that melts a man's heart. I couldn't move my eyes away, she was aware of my thought because my eyes were talking for me, seemed like she was watching me as I was lusting on her beauty, she was sexy, different from anything I had loved before. We made eye contact again, but just a brief eye contact.

I followed her, watched those legs move so sexily down the hallway, her sashay was like a fingerprint in my mind, damn that looks so good, love to witness them silk panties she said she likes buying here. "Hell, hey baby Girl!" I said, "Can I buy them sexy silk panties you said you have a fascination of? Hell, me too! All you have to do is call me when you put them on and I will buy you a shit load of them sexy panties", but she said, "I can buy my own", She licked her lips. I smelled the sweetness of her perfume and the freshness of her breath, her voice sounded sexy like she looks but she didn't look like she was from either world I live in, the project or the dope game. Her clear fingernails, diamond earrings or bling bling, a pretty expensive watch on, my mind keep going sideways over and over like I had some sort of a nervous tic, like my mac conversation is played out.

Her expression remained unreadable, she had straight teeth and a sexy shaped face, and her breasts looked like they hadn't been offended by a man's gravity, like someone has not yet put them in their mouth and suck them one at a time. Her youth was an aphrodisiac to a man's sexual desires or pleasures, and she knew it too. I asked her, "What's your name?"

"Shimin!" I told her that people call me T-Mac, Shimin said, "You think you're a player or something, calling yourself T-Mac?" "No, Shimin! I'm like the big mac sandwich from McDonalds", she gave me two thumbs up, her laugh ended up with a big nice smile that carried to her eyes. Her nose was small, her lips were full of beauty, the one you can just kiss on the first date and you will love her. I was trying to decide if I was going to lie, if she asks me if I have a girlfriend, Shimin asked, "How old are you?" "I'm twenty!" then I had a good look at her soft tan skin, skin that I had touched before, a hard memory having the act, capacity, or function of mentally reproducing and recognizing previous or past experience, could it be that Shimin reminds me of Gigi? Being my own desires, found myself being a young man in need of a new love that made me look at Shimin in an all new way, I try to dissect her beautiful features, I asked, "Shimin, you're part white and part black huh, Shimin?" "Yes! T-Mac I am, what's your real name? I know your parents didn't name you T-Mac, how can we be a close acquaintance if I don't know your real name, I think that not a good idea do you think so?"

She has undergone a big change to make a conversation to one's own use which is hers. Is she worthy of the name, my character that belongs to me are the thing in question, to change property from real to personal, for us to join or separate. Hell, I know her game, her check-call so it looked like a champion, you know, to get what she wants. She's a player who takes advantage of a situation to get maximum value, well I am too! "Shimin, my real name is T-Mac." She trusts the name, the most potent and inspiring her heart for one of a kind mass and strength to build her trust and supplement the world of love, she has never seen. I'm going to rock her nutrition mac-ing, having a development to feed in her little game. Sometimes I can be a nutshell, the mac shell enclosing the meat of a nut, sometimes I feel like a nut, and sometime I am. Now players! They're gonna rock your own mac brand that works,

"T-Mac!" she said "I like your name, I'm not going to call you T-Mac, I think your real name's sexy!" I faced her, took all her words eye-to-eye. She's being hypothetical, her accent had turned in to a Spanish accent when she said my name. I asked her how far she had to travel to get back home, she said, "I live three blocks away, I walked up here, do you know where Elm Street is? Well, that's the street where I live at T-Mac." I thought to myself, it's all about reading people, finding out what I need to know, this is the shit I'm talking about! Hell, Shimin practically told me her address, all I have to do is go to that damn street, she calls the street name Elm, hell, the motion picture, "Nightmare on Elm Street", I hope her ass is not related to Freddy Krueger. You know if she doesn't give me her phone number, my ass will be sitting in my car, looking stupid to see her walk down the street, to know where she is staying, you know. If I get the detonating explosives "No! you can't have my phone number!" There was a Noo In my mind to separate between joy and sorrow! There, by opening the circuit for me to be staking her, and Freddy Krueger will come out and get my ass! "Hey, Shimin can a brother get your seven digits? I will only call you everyday that's all." She laughed at that, she didn't agree but she laughed, she said, "I was supposed to go hook up with my new friend when I leave here T-Mac!" That was a game she was playing on me, I can feel that shit was a lie, trust me! My truth begets truthful, I lowered my mac game, you know, not talking so fast but thinking before speaking. I can admit I'm no virgin at this making, did she just admit that she was little

Red Riding Hood, on her little sexy way to her boyfriend's house? I said, "I don't know where you and I stood, I only want to give you this number, because I only want to do right!" Shimin said, "I don't understand what you mean when you say that you only want to do right!" "Yes, Shimin! When he fucks up, I'm one phone call away, to do right by you and you better not have both of us!" I told her she was more than welcome to crash at my truth, you see, a woman is more attractive to a man when they can't figure them out. Yes, lock down in their mind that you are not a cheater because I told her she can't have both of us. She looked at me, knowing. You know player! The look you get when you got them! A few people stopped and checked the table of sexy women and others moved on. She cranked up a sexy harsh smile as she came towards me, my eyes went to her right hand, it's something about me that excites a woman and makes them want to do things they know they shouldn't be doing. I call it anyway, to make them move to strong emotions! She reached into her purse, showed me her ink pen that was in her right hand, it was the kind that you can flip open. "I like your little cute pen Shimin", she wrote down a phone number in fire red ink and handed it to me. "Area code 619, Oh thank you T-Mac! This is my favorite ink pen!" I said "O, thank you Shimin, this is my favorite phone number because it comes from your favorite pen!" Help me pick me a favorite ink pen, so I can give you my number Shimin". You catching game player! Make her feel she had something to do with that special number she just put in her cute little purse.

Oh yes! She's going to call it. Real player! Are you talking to me? The traffic light changed right back to green, a woman's game is the shit! Jeanette is right, she gave me a player game! Ha...Ha...Ha..."

You feel me? Shimin is an encouraging angel, a sign from above. "When I say love you to you, it is not my heart that speaks, it's the priest from Grego", he whispered gesturing at the phone, "E-Tar". She sighed and turned off the radio. Q- Loc, he was kind of hot for E-Tar doing that shit, "E-Tar, tell the right reverend, Hello!" She said to Grego and he had to put a finger in his cauliflower ear to hear what Trish was saying on the phone. I heard about this mess but let me fill you in on this game, Grego is a real player, he's the only one of us who has two girlfriends under one roof at the same time and the love team with the most right orgasm climax or participatory hokeypokey wins a baby! E-Tar, she turned to Grego, he sat on the bed with his head down, face in his hands. His missing heart looked normal to her now, she ran her fingers through his oily black hair, "Baby?" She said, "That bitch Trish is saying she is pregnant with you Grego! That's what everybody is talking about." Grego needs a sign, a sign from above. Grego looked over at E-Tar, and said "What kind of stupid question is that E- Tar, how in the hell will I know? It's like saying, maybe money grows on trees or maybe pennies fall from heaven." E-Tar said, "Maybe it does, Grego!" A woman plays an upright role, while a man shouts into an "I don't give a fuck" role. "I have faith in you, E-Tar" said Grego.

It wasn't until after he realized the rarefied company Trish puts him in, a more natural hurt than knowledge. The whole purpose of nature embodied in a woman is that she can enslave a man. "I'm having your baby!" To have the chief in the creator of her little world of I love you! Your partner opens one heart and you buy two diamonds and she rebinds two hearts. Man, she got your ass! I hope you have an emergency coverage plan, we don't cover extravagance player! If you'd like to upgrade to our premium membership, we'll cover luxuries like ambulances, bandages and oxygen when she takes your ass to the bank, remember the last time someone gave her a real dollar bill or even a diamond ring like your dumb ass just did, a green pickup passed slowly, and in the back of it said, "Trick Daddy! Til' Death Do Us Part!" But if her love points the way to heaven, no one has to tell you that you found your love!

Jeanette knew we were drifting apart, and she begins to do voodoo on me. One day, Jeanette called me up at the dope spot telling me she cooked me a special dinner, my favorite spaghetti! I was sitting at the table having a strong craving for some spaghetti, she always cook it the way I love it. To a man's eager desire, I was hungry, well, high too. "T-Mac! T-Mac!" Kiana said, she was standing in the hallway door in the kitchen, I looked at her and my eyes went back to my plate of spaghetti on the table that Jeanette just put down, steaming hot. I looked back at Kiana because she was buzzing like a bee! Buzz, buzz, buzz. It was Sharon, April, Myesha, and Kiana still buzzing like a bee, all of them pretty girls sashayed back and forth, smiling my way, the answer to that look they were giving me costs more than I could afford. Then it all came to me in a flash, they were trying to tell me something that they didn't want Jeanette to know, so I walked out of the kitchen to their bedroom. Myesha closed the door behind them, it became one big buzz of conversations all around me, I couldn't understand what they were saying because all of them were talking at the same time, I said, "Hold on! Stop it, just wait a minute!" They stopped talking. Sharon put her soft hands on my arms, I hate to think of the things she had to say, the closer we got to the truth, each step broke my heart, I didn't understand Jeanette and wasn't ready for that kind of crazy temporary passion but we lived in different worlds, at least we did in my mind. After the girls told me what's up, I knew how I felt about Jeanette's lifestyle. She knew because when I came out of the girls' bedroom, I looked uncomfortable, both pissed off and ashamed of loving her. Without a word, I grabbed my coat, put my car keys in my hand and I followed the girls towards the front door thinking about blood-soaked spaghetti. Jeanette put her menstruation in my plate of spaghetti, damn she is on her period today. With the pain in my head and the chronic smoke and alcohol in my bloodstream, that shit Sharon and the girls told me were the last thing a brother needs to hear. What you said, you know, about being lonely. Shimin's sexy soft voice followed me all the way to Dever Fever's house, there's only two kinds of trouble in this world, Love trouble and money trouble. A mac can't come across having love problems, I'm going with the money problems, that's why I'm headed to the dope spot at Dever Fever driving in my Cadillac, dressed in all black. Hell, when I'm crying on my carphone to Shimin how lonely I am for a long time, I didn't say anything, didn't think I was supposed to. After she ended her little speech, she hit me with a cold line! Shimin said, "Don't get dead on me, you're a nice guy T-Mac!

Remember you told me, you will call every day? I don't hear my phone ringing, do you?" She made a phone sound ring with her voice, "Ring, ring, ring", and said, "Hello! Oh hi! T-Mac baby!" The thing about a young girl was that if you talked to her young ass long enough, you will realize that she was still a little daddy's girl, she might have her mature moments, but somewhere along her line of thoughts digressed from the shit you're trying to get across, it reflexive to the shit you really give a fuck about for all my twenty years on earth. But I love the shit we discussed about all the men she met who either try to controll her by buying her things like L.A. Gear and FILA Sport and Adidas shoes to handbag accessories, Oh yeah! To those sexy silk underwire like I said I would buy if she calls me when she puts them on, and pricey diamond jewelry, the entire stock capris and skimmers from Lee and Gloria Vanderbilt, she had on that day I met her. Those Lee was hugging her ass, and the sexy legs hanging out those blue jeans and fine fragrances, Donna Karen and she had a pair of Gazelle like me, if your sunglasses were not Gazelle, you're ass is not shit. Man,

thinking all about this shit I wonder what her sleepwear is, or she sleeps in nothing? All this to say, men buy her things because they want her pussy, she never found love, I can just feel it. Somehow, I'm loving her. She said, "You're the best guy I've ever talked to on the phone T-Mac, it's like you know what a woman is feeling or wht she needs to hear, not like most men thinking they are cool. To hear beautiful things like you do makes me feel so good."

"Dog gone good". I said "That's your wild ass", she said. "What makes a man feel so damn good without a kiss, can I have one Shimin?" She said, "How am I going to give you one over the phone?" I was smiling because I got her where I want her, "Yes you can Shimin!" "How can I do that T-Mac!" "Like this Shimin! Mmmmwahhhh!" I made a kiss sound over the phone with my voice and Shimin was eating it up, when Shimin blew back a kiss over the phone, it made me draw my own conclusion about her full but sexy lips making the letter O kiss for me, her fresh breath and beautiful teeth.

Shimin was cool, a great girlfriend if I can get her to say she will be mine, but she was the kind I'd get serious about because I still have fantasies of some lovely trustworthy beautiful young lady who come stumbling into my lonely world. I fell into the arms of nurturing girls who played shitty game. I focused on pleasure instead of pain, the little headed for self- mutilation when you are in love it hurts so good, but in the end, so hard to let go. I felt some sort of a need to connect to my past ex-lover, I closed my eyes tight to see their ghost faces in my past and not all ghosts were all bad. I can remember the ghosts faces of both my parents sitting in my high school stand at my track meet, I would look over at the stands and wish that my parents were there to see me run a race, to really see how spectacular their son really was, not just at my school but in the whole world. Shimin's pheromones made me lose control of my thought. "Shimin, you are sexy as hell." I had to trust myself and stop holding back my feelings for her. "Can I be your Big Mac sandwich and you take a big bite out of me, you know! A Scooby-Doo snack, I'm a jellified Happy Meal." She was laughing her sexy butt out and said, "How much would it cost me?" I said, "Good faith money Shimin, that's all!" She said, "What does that mean, T-Mac?" "Oh, that you promise to be my girlfriend. It costs pretty much that! And for the flower toy, it costs extra, I hope you don't mind." She said, "T-Mac, how much extra?" I said, "A real kiss extra!" She said, "I think I can afford that T-Mac!" We agreed, it felt pleasant and I was willing to make our relationship work, hell, I feel a lot better, like the Italian would say, "I feel relievo!" Yes! My heart felt relieved about our conversation.

I was still sitting in my car talking to Shimin on my carphone in front of the spot, I can see Stephon's head peeping through the front door glass window curious why I was sitting in the car so long. He knew I always come in the spot fast when I pull up. "Hold on Shimin! My cousin Stephon is coming to my car!" "Okay", she said. "T-Mac!" Stephon said, "Are you all right?" "Yes, Stephon I'm cool brother!" "Oh, I know your ass always comes in fast T-Mac, all right! Be careful out here, one time is hot!" "All right love one", I said, "Hey, Shimin! Are you still there?" "Yes babe!" But she quickly went to work on me with most practiced dexterity and within an hour I'd done her better justice, though it was all I could do to keep up with her, hell, she was doubled-jointer everywhere, she had me fooled, she was witty! I know now! Man, I remember telling her, she can take a bite out of the big mac, not eat the whole burger! I didn't know what she was talking about, but I sighed with admiration at her selflessness, "Shimin!" I said, "What do you mean it doesn't matter? It matters now more than ever", Shimin said, "I'm not blaming you for not answering your phone because I have been calling that number the same day you gave it to me. I help you pick your favorite pin for you to give me your phone number, I thought you stood me up T-Mac and gave me a fake number." I said, "I don't mean to suggest that the number is fake, Shimin! It's my car phone number", talking about the truth with a woman was supposed to be an act of spiritual enlightenment, embodying a kind of dream love when everything became one mind out of two minds believing in one another, "Yes", I said, recovering my breath, "That's right, Shimin. Now, I will show you that I have a car" She said, "You can come over to my house, this is my address, do you get it? Yes! That's it, right babe on Elm Street. Okay, you got it, how long would it take for you to get to my house? Okay, I will be looking out for you! Oh, babe, what kind of car do you have for I will be outside looking out for you? A Cadillac? You're lying ha...ha... ha... T-Mac! You're Lying if your ass won't be here in twenty minute, I'm calling you back at that number you gave me, and if you don't answer, I'm going to be mad at you T-Mac." I said, "Why do you have to call me back Shimin?" "Because I know you are lying T-Mac about you having a car, and especially a Cadillac!" "No! Shimin Not that! I told you I'm in my car talking to you on my car phone. I get really attached to people,tThe wrong girl for the right reasons, I guess that's just the way I'm made." She laughed at me, I don't have control of my emotion barometer and antinomy, the contradiction between Shimin and me about me being a liar.

Damn, there's a million street names I have seen but not hers. In my mind I was thinking, she was love hurt and has been lied to, and lonely, like myself too. She was a passenger on that same bumpy as road, well I can say other people have bigger problems who needs me, some outstanding questions, even if they had the power to go ahead to make the reparations in their lives how when Black people are manacled by low- quality schools, higher rates of such social illness and sickness like Aids and drug addiction, that end up to many broken families. Maybe that doesn't matter to the dope slanger like me and the nasty hoes, we all set on making our lives in a green- horn. A few seconds later, my thoughts were back in my head, so was my life crossword puzzle I just had put in my pocket. Get your paper man! By all means necessary! Oh, you people too even if you are on the right track, you will get run over if you hear every word that life has to toss you, loud and clear! Hey asshole! This is so powerful that I can hear your conversation from across the street. Just remember this, taking all your doses and paying less, that's the shit I'm talking about! But both make us feel good! Just remember that! "Okay, Shimin! I'm on Imperial and Euclid, I remember make a Left, yes Shimin! You told me when I see Bear Market make a left". Shimin said, "Before you get to the flea market, where I met you at, that traffic light you will see Bear market on the Left, so make that left there, remember I told you, I live three streets down from Flea Market?"

"Yes, Shimin, I remember!" "Okay, T-Mac! You will see a Taco Bell to the right, as soon as you pass Taco Bell, the first street to the right is

Elm and I told you the street Elm go to a fork in the road, my house is on the right in the fork in the road, well T-Mac, I will be outside okay!" "All right, Shimin!" "Goodbye Babe!" "Babe Girl! It's not goodbye, it's see you later!" She said, "Fast later!"

I knew the ramification, it will be a really powerful exercise, these finances of life are economically self-sufficient, but we so much desire these finances or the necessities of life, I'm having self-determination. In fact, they stood shoulder to shoulder in the feelings Shimin and I are having, the best solution is to tell Jeanette it's over after that shit she pulled on me, it's no discrimination about whose sexier, it's about unified black brother leadership but there was a unity of mission in my heart for Jeanette, like the day the world stood still when the shit happens. You know the saying, "Slippin on your pimpin", player! The most valuable truth, I will not speak that truth to poor Jeanette, she's looking for the light of the promised land in God's heaven above, while she's still on earth, she will not get any pain from me! Therefore my heart rejoiced, my love for her was made gladden and if a brother tries to break the spell of love by suggesting we move beyond those ancient of ex-lovers and tried tactics, they are put down with language that implicates them as fools in the player hate establishment. Reactionaries who've forgotten their root to feel oneself as a martyr, as everybody knows, is a pleasurable thing, to marvel the fact that we came through this lifetime safely is a wonderful thing, as developing love for one another! The mass- energy relationship of the special theory of relativity, I have to be a floor pad to protect Jeanette's little heart. Love assassination killed that idea as well.

Shimin told me her street is right after Taco Bell, and there it goes! Elm Streem, where my new lover lives near, so I cranked up my monger sounds, 4-18" woofers with the tweets, 600-1000 watt amps. Shimin can hear my shit from here by Taco Bell. There she is with her mouth open, her eyes unbelieving to what she see, the true confession. She is so damn sexier than the first time I met her, then an idea pops up into my head, well a wish actually! I was walking along the beach, finds a lantern and rubs it, a genie pops out and says, "Thank you for releasing me, as a reward I will grant you any wish your heart desires." "Great," I said, "First of all, we got to make your ass a black man, I want a girl who can cook, a girl who's great-looking named Shimin, and a girl who's crazy sexy in bed."

"Anything else brother?" "Yeah! genie brother! I don't want them to ever find out about each other." Ha...Ha...Ha... Because Jeanette will try to kill both of them, Shimin's sexy fine self, you think I forgot about my "fuck me in my ass" freak bitch? Hell no! "Hello, ladies!" "Shimin, who's your friend?" "Hi! T-Mac whichever one." "Little momma, it can be two." "You mean both?" "No, little momma! Two, like two scoops of ice cream, can I have both of them?! You see little momma, if it's both, that means you two are my girlfriends, the two in both!" "Hahaha, Shimin, he's funny! Ahh, did you just say I had fungus feet? Jokes on you little momma." She ended her big laughter with "You're a really nice guy. Cute and funny. Do you have a friend for me?" Her and Shimin, are by far one of the baddest I ever graced my eyes on. I only need a suck for loved ones, but real talk I'd love to be both of them lollipops. So thank God for giving me some play with Miss Candi's sweets angels! Oh, well, dammit when I wanna get nasty. I said, "Little momma!" She said, "That's not my name!" "Hold up! Little momma, I like that name, besides, someone's mofucking mom can be ugly and their asses will still love there momma! You see little momma why your nickname is perfect for you? A nigga might look at you and think about his mom because your nickname is Little momma and he will start to love your ugly ass, beside I don't hook up with ugly people like you. Hell Little momma, don't you think that we already have enough ugly babies in the world?" If you know how much laugher costs in the store, you can imagine how much that stuff costs from the look she was giving me, but Shimin I think had no more funny bone left because she was laughing so hard that she was gasping for air. To break that cold as ice look on little momma face, I said, "Little momma," "Don't play with me T-Mac!" Little momma said. "Hold up!Extremely sexy Little momma! Are you mad at your boy? I'm just saying, why do a mac makes you wanna hate him, but you love him in the end! I keep bringing you a game to the table and I will be a subscriber for life. Wow! You fickle one problem, and it always solves another one." Shimin had a jealous look on her face for calling her friend extremely sexy! I thought it would be a typical Friday evening but when things start to get interesting on Elm Street, I presume you probably knows this, so for the sake of not debating the first amendment and keeping things right (tis the love season) I'll say this: "Shimin, you are the most outshining beautiful woman I've ever seen in the world!" "Unless, Little momma is from another Galaxy, I will be all right!" "Shimin, as an early Christmas present. Just don't take these flowers I bought for you under the mistletoe, believe it or not, Shimin off-the-hook made-up her own mind to lay one on me. I just got invited into a first time playground kiss and it was hard to unplug ourselves, our lips moved slowly and easy, my eyes went to her. There was hotness in her eyes, like saying "It's longing!" I kissed someone so hot, so warm that my coldness went away. She told me, "I want you so bad daddy!" "I could tell. Damn, I could tell!" Daddy haven't had sex in at least…. Skirter!

Skirter… okay it went like this! I handed her the flowers, she smiled and said "Thank you T-Mac! Can you cut off your sounds because my daddy is in the house?" I'm in one of them similarities I cannot always win an argument, every time someone tells me to turn down my mongers sounds, I turn it up! You know the shit your grandmother has all that old shit sitting on the shelves on the wall, those old ass are called antiques! I will get rid of all that shit in the wall for you, my sounds will shake that shit off the walls in your houses! "Damn! T-Mac, I can finally hear myself talking!" All in all, it was a type of smart talk Shimin had, she said "I know this not your Cadillac T-Mac!" She put her smart card on my table to see what kind of man I was, I asked myself why I would fall in the little game she's playing, why bother working my mind over nothing and in addition to that, I'm off that chronic smoke side effect from drinking to drunken and I was in a pretty foul mood. She said these words twice: "Don't get dead on me!" and that's the time I felt my luck was so bad. If it was raining pussy,

I would be the only one to get hit in the head with a dick, but hell, I was thinking this is not like the shit Jeanette tried to pull on me so I put on my player game face and went to my car to grab the keys and my car registration to Dollar. Shimin is really good because her ass is smart and a little crazy and she's sexy too. Her beauty is overwhelming and her body is magnificent, we can get in the tub in the shower and wish I was just one drop of that water running over Shimin's beautiful 36-24-46 frame. I'm sure any flavour of ice cold water would quench the thirst! So good, so right! I guess Shimin's life was all about showing your lifestyles, be rich or be shameless in her eyes! After seeing my car registration she said, "Big things poppin, huh T-Mac?!" I said, "All cool like little something! Brother would like to from the hood dollar to Hollywood! Sit back relax, and check this Flyness out! Move the buckets for me to glide through traffic people!"

Why is your ass rolling your eyes at Dollar? That's the shit Ms. Dollar does, she's an eye looker or a hooker. When she sits on a street corner, niggas will be acting like they got their paper and say "Hey homie! It's for sale." Everywhere Ms. Dollar passes from one place to another or depart, niggas are very much the same but very different. Oh, I don't tell Shimin how some niggas fear Ms. Dollar! Passion of lust! That's what she is "Dollar, dollar bill" Not that I speak in regards to me for I have learned that in whatever state of mind I'm in, I have to be content. I know how to be a hustler but I'm not standing on no corner, and for what? I get my money!

Everywhere and in all things, I'd learned both to be full and to be hungry. I grew up in the project, I'm sure that everyone else too in the hood, so it makes me almost a fatalist on some levels. In the hood, a nigga calls a brother like me a Baller to be accessible. Like me, you have to reach a point that you get rich or die trying. Niggas got into altercation in this hustling game and some lost their lifts to the streets! I mean, the past just brings back hurting memories to me. Going back to the project, seeing old faces and knowing that you will never see some of them again hurt so much. No one gets to be successful over night and then having it taken away from you, it's pretty much like dying! The only thing missing from the dope game is: IQ test! If you're smart, your ass knows better not to make a statement!

Shimin calls me by the name my mother named me to make herself feel like she's on a different level, because everybody benefits on different thoughts. Shimin is not trying to throw shots at me or hurt me in any way... I made a big mistake in my life because on some levels, it comes from me coming from where I came from, the project! "T-Mac!" Shimin said "I keep on thinking to myself in my head, I had to keep my thoughts to myself because I almost forgot to tell you." My player reparations movement is a flashy distraction from the real ideas, what I come here for and what I need to do is take advantage of the opportunities, to get a real kiss from her, finding a way towards her truth, would she put her... It was a conversation Shimin just had out loud to herself, she said laughing, "I think my dad must be fun. He is. Okay, I gotta go!" Her dad's voice came from inside the house!

"Girl! Get in the house! Who's that boy?" "My friend daddy!"

"Well, tell him to go! And get your butt in here!"

"Okay Daddy! T-Mac, I have to go in the house but tomorrow we can hang out, because my dad will be at work!" She said that in a low whisper! Backwards, backwards. The Ability to take is backwards, slow motion! People, come on! Are you following me? I hope so because my name tag is on this shit, that plastic attached to something or hung from the wearer's neck for the purpose of identification, or you can say: classification! Damn! But her dad Price tag said "5.0 or get up! Get down! 911 is a joke in your town!" Shimin's Dad was standing in the front doorway of his house, in his cop uniform!

Bottom dollar slang means the last of one's money, bet one's bottom dollar! Hell, the bottom line or the end result of all this shit is: How in the hell can a dope dealer and a cop be friends? This is not the first trumpet I've played! Yes officer, I do! Like your ass is marrying that mofucker or something. I do, you know? Those plastic tags that says, identification please! It's my pleasure sir! Talking like a Greek. Artful downs well when the pigs run your name, your ass will go to jail like the people held for minor offenses or pending judicial proceedings. I can say, I'm cool! I mean, not on Shimin, hell no! I'm not here to be her daddy's friend, I'm here for Shimin who's sexy and beautiful, all in one. Shimin is the apple of my eyes, the dream of my heart. A girl all boys love to have on their arms, she is a man's dream, right player! Okay, you might have the exception of a few who make it their duties or responsibilities to say they only love one girl. Sssh! Hey man! There's a voice saying, I know why you are saying that's your woman right there. Oh, last week she was a bitch! That's right! It was cold and you're sitting your ass outside the house with all the little shit your ass moves in with all the overfly shit you had on, thinking your ass was Fly Daddy talking to the other sexy dream girl you think a handsome player like you deserves with your broke ass!

Your real ugly woman, she had just tossed all your shit outside in the trash! Hell! That was what it was in the first place! Come on, now you know I'm right! Oh, I don't mean to front you off, well, like she just did! Hell that's goes for me too, not the broke shit but my Ballers for Ballers brand tag I pay big money for, you feel me? Jeanette knows better not to fuck with a brother's clothes! You see women, don't be thinking your brother, man, or nigga! Don't be thinking about your ass when he's out there fucking up! Well, okay! Like this: "Come on babe please don't break my shit! It's not like that baby, come on babe, please believe me, it's not like that, I Love you Babe! Please babe, don't break my shit!"

All right Lattys, you win! I see now that negros only think about their shit and not your love, but lady, will you toss the Mac shit out or break it? I don't want to stick around to see the outcome of that shit lady! I have pains too that take me backwards! Look Lady, take French lessons, use the French word "Chien" which means dog, well, sometimes being a dog is worth it! I mean, Shimin's sexy lips are right on. Oh, I'm sure it got ugly, really ugly. She's still whispering in my ear, kissing my neck, okay you got me! Her sexy lips touching my ear, her breasts have been offended by the gravity of my arm, and smacked a loud kiss, one that no one can separate our lips, or you can say, her lips from my ear. She still whispers low in my ear, her warm fresh breath, her sexy voice, and her lips are on my earlobe, her body on my right arm is so soft, her breasts are still on my arm. My heart is so cold and so hurt, but full of love, cold love, because love is pain, old pain we hold on to. Letting go is something we tell ourselves all the time, but it keeps on coming back.

The new green love gardens are beautiful, the green light in our minds that think like a waterless rock garden, became a mind-set. I don't have to put that much effort in this relationship because I'm not going to not get hurt in this time in life, the thought in our heads fuck you up all the time huh? Hell, I know it does for me, any plum that may be or has been dried without fermentation. Take the fear out of pruning! Notwithstanding love lost in thought, but you have anxious care, you know? My little head is talking to me, uhuh, my little head is telling me, "You're hooorrnnyy! Little mammo is on Fire!" I know you know the shit I'm talking about, that goes on between her legs! Woman! Or is it my mind playing tricks on me.

I feel a new growth, the growth just as it is sending nutrients and energy into the reserves for the cold months ahead. Not only can valuable reserves be diverted back into new growth, new love! Yes, can this be? She is whispering in my ear, she loves to run off with me tomorrow and be daddy's little bad girl, but the old cops see it in his daughter's eyes that she is in love with a hustler or a thug! Oh, I am not! Not me! I'm a dead flower in Daddy cop's eyes. The way he looks at me in the eyes while Shimin is still whispering in my ear. Poppo can see Shimin telling me something that his baby girl doesn't like daddy to know! Daddy cop's eyes are pruning in necessary to control size or power, to remove dead or diseased branches or limbs, to improve structure or to stimulate new groeth or flowering his daughter's love. Hell, people you know are right there in the growth of eve, the evenings mean a day preceding a special day, such as a Saint's day or holiday. But when it is a man to man period of looking each other in the eyes, it is immediately preceding a certain event: the eve of war. You see, this can be especially true for Evergreen houses you have, the damage could also create access points for over-wintering pests and diseases. He thinks about me, as cops get paid to do, to put a nigga like me in jail and keep all this fantasy out of his beautiful daughter who is hotter and sexier than anyone else.

Shimin said, "Now remember T-Mac, I'm going to call you so be by your car phone when I call tomorrow about 8:00, okay? Or you can call me, I will be up at 6:00 in the morning, okay T-Mac?"

"Yes Shimin", I said. The poppo's eye ball are looking at my dollar license plate! This old cop from the cop business establishment calls his partner at work to get the get down on me. Ha ha ha, but I have not been in your devilish computer ever before, and never will pig! Who said a nigga can't be a farmer too?

Tomorrow, I'm fucking farming his daughter! Believe me, Shimin is feeling me. We armed ourselves with dignity and self-respect. The greatness of this period is that we straightened our backs up for tomorrow, and believe in love that has determination. I must assume primary responsibility to make it work! I received a note that identified himself as a cop or a civil rights leader and as he puts it, he is at the top of his field. In speaking out, he presents himself as an ordinary man with a deep passion for the well-being of the law of the people by the people, but not black people. He is full of rage of an average man who sees vulnerable people being hurt and feels compelled to speak out about it, not to lure into harm or hurt, but the love only a father knows for a daughter. When young people, and older people take on a spirit of rebellion in our clothes, language, music, and other forms of expression, her daddy eyes me like a black underclass Negro.

Pretty soon, you're going to have to present DNA cards so you can tell who you're making love to, which would be cool because I'm only thinking about her only. I would wish all the others away for Shimin's love, she's like the summer breeze in the winter's coldest season. Shimin is my summer, when the sun sets, her smile makes no better feeling than the sunshine on a dark day. Her sexy sunflower face smiles sunrise in her sexy green eyes that shines in my eyes telling me to go for a kiss pertaining to an "I love you". The sun is shining brightly in my mind, and sex was not something I was thinking about as I look into her eyes, I know I loved her so much.

It is a subject that never fails to fascinate me, to love someone and not get hurt over and over again, something I knew well to a point that I could not get it off my mind. I made a promise to myself. Shimin is doing a lot of careful planning in my ear, and I love it. We said our goodbyes or like I always say, later.

"Jeanette, are you sure you don't feel ill?" Jeanette said, "No, not a bit. It's just that it's such a pleasure to have you here with me T-Mac." I said, "Well Jeanette, I'm going to be at the spot", and Jeanette couldn't help but notice a distinct in my voice on the phone. Jeanette said, "I wish you wouldn't do me like that T-Mac". "Like what, Jeanette?" "You know what I'm talking about T-Mac, I know I need to change the game I'm playing with you baby, only because I love you and I'm feeling I'm losing you to someone new T-mac. Never mind Babe." But I can't imagine any other reason she's be acting like that, "You'd better change your mind on that shit Jeanette", I said with a hearty laugh, at least in her own mind Jeanette thinks her love spells or voodoo are going to work on me, to stop me from seeing Shimin, but Jeanette is good, she know there's someone I've been seeing, clearly something is going on in her big head, I had to think about this. I waved aside her apologies, unless my heart is mistaken, which is not, she is fucked up, and I would say the unthinkable will take place today. I'm very grateful that the girls told me, I assumed I have no choice, I've got to work on a lot of things though. The reality of it was just beginning to sink in my mind, there's something about Jeanette that bothers me. From what I understand, she would keep a hawk's watch on her investment, which is me. I had to be careful never to be caught going to Ocean view with Shimin in the car.

Jeanette asked "Is someone with you T-Mac?",

I said. "No, I'm alone, I just got here at Dever Fever's spot, why Jeanette?"

"I'm just asking, that's all. Babe, where have you been? And have you come up with any answers to the things you said were bothering you T-Mac?"

"Yes Jeanette, you have a lot of questions and I cannot help you with that Jeanette!"

"Babe!" Jeanette said, "I'm here for you, just remember that if you want to talk to someone."

"I'll remember Jeanette",

She said, "I was wondering if I could stop by and see you later this afternoon T-Mac. I think Dever Fever would not mind." "Of course Jeanette, you can come and see me. Has something come up?"

"No, T-Mac! I'm missing you, that's all. Have you eaten something baby?"

"Yes, I have Jeanette. Is that all right?"

"Babe, I know you love my cooking and you can still eat my food. I will not put anything in your food, no more okay?"

I was not trying to listen to what Jeanette was saying. She knows that I am trying to overhear what she's saying, she raised her voice slightly, "I apologize T-Mac, okay! I could give you so many examples babe, but I'm not okay!"

"All right, Jeanette! I'll see you in a while."

"Okay, babe", Jeanette said, "And may I bring someone with me, is that all right?"

"Yes, Jeanette it's all right."

We hung up at the end of her call, she was making me feel like a king, asking me if she can bring someone. Jeanette knows damn well that she would do what the fuck she likes to do. You feel me! This is the shit I'm talking about, she needs something that would help me separate her bullshit from love. She asked if I had eaten because her ass must have been blowing up my car phone when I was at Shimin's house. Man, Shimin's sexy voice is still ringing in my ear, can I keep it real with her and tell her about Jeanette? Hell, I'm moving too fast, Shimin and I are just friends, that's all.

I tend to look for all the possibilities when I'm trying to solve a problem. Hell, it will be a problem when Jeanette finds out about Shimin, I'll make sure it wouldn't happen. I thought about it but I can't stand blood and

I'm not too crazy about dead bodies. Jeanette had a perfect opportunity to make things right by me and she fucked up, and she will be coming to the dope spot to ask me if we can have sex, I know her. Yes, I'm going to back down on her ass, I'm thinking about tomorrow and yes Shimin and I are going out together. She has such a sexy smile too, but she wouldn't mind stealing a night of sweaty sex, only her conscience stands in her way, Shimin's dad. Unfortunately, tomorrow he's not going to be there, I thought the idea was to make our harvest love honey because she's the new bee in my life, that has to be a delicate operation to start with. I'm just trying to find the love of my life, some logical explanation for all of this. A little set back with Jeanette because she doesn't think of me as a concerned individual, put her menstruation in my plate of spaghetti and if the electricity happened to go out, my nigga will laugh at me for a week. It doesn't matter, tomorrow they will see how fine Shimin is back by the man. I was the mac, hell I'm still the mac, I have women putting shit in my food to put a spell on me to keep me their man, that shit is crazy as hell. Shimin will pull me away from all this mess.

I see Stephon looking out the door at me with a big smile on his face. Hell, news gets around fast. I need fresh air to clear out all the shit I had in my head recently, I can't believe I almost get blown up by Jeanette's so called love spell. I should have figured it out sooner. I remember our pit bull Cocaine, dig up one of my favorite pair of boxers in the yard, the girls told me Jeanette buried them in the ground. I was wondering why it was hard for me to leave the house, all this time Jeanette was doing her love spells and voodoo on me, she had to derail my train of thought, well, my love for her because there was no relief in sight making me her Hussy, her butt doing that where anybody can see. I feel responsible, I should have identified our love the first day I had eyes for Kiana, and now she is a stepdaughter and not a lover. Would Shimin be in my life if Kiana was my lover? I like having the answers in my head. Yes, I'm very turned on thinking about having two pretty girls in my mind, right player! To kiss the living daylights out of them, I always wondered what that expression meant, and now, thanks to Jeanette, she knew. As I kissed her the way I do, shot out of her like sparks from a gun but she had her fingers on the trigger and I'm the victim. You can take that to the bank, you can bet her tongue is massaging my tonsils like crazy, rubbing all over me, sucking my face and rubbing our bodies like lovers or something. It wasn't supposed to turn out that way, and she began to heat up all over. Jeanette could probably defrost Frosty the snowman between her thighs with no problem. Not to mention the hottest mouth I ever stuck my tongue into.

Cool as I could be, I walked in the spot before I can get to the front door, I can smell the weed smoke. Stephon opened the door and I walked inside. "Does it smell funny in here or do we smell period or spaghetti?" Q-Loc said in a joking, laughing voice. "All right ya'll! You got me", I said. Grego looked at me like saying, "I told you that woman was a mad crazy woman", but he couldn't tell what. Her expression had always been open but to him, this is the far most crazy thing Jeanette had done, he wanted to know why. "What's the sudden unforeseen in Jeanette?", Grego's voice sounded slightly strangled, like he might be trying not to laugh. I know it sounds blow, but in actuality it's extremely likely he might be trying not to laugh. He glanced over at E-Tar, I'm feeling more like a fool every minute. I will not admit that, I'm being very disloyal to my making if I do, I suppose I'm very good at this shit, something was going on with E-Tar, but I couldn't tell what. She has always been open, but now she wasn't. She seems to be hiding something, "Do you mind if I say something, T-Mac?", E-Tar said. "No, E-Tar go ahead," Hell, what more can hurt, I was thinking, it's not like a food mart might stock magazines with my face on the cover, eating a big plate of Jeanette's spaghetti for the whole world to know. Nothing could disgust me more than that. "Okay, T-Mac", she scrunched up her face and covered her knees, she smiled at me and said, "I see you are still wrong about that, T-Mac, no one's going to laugh at you when I tell you this T-Mac. You need to watch your back babe because Jeanette has lost her mind doing that to a man. She thinks that's the only way to keep a man, by putting her nasty menstruation period in a man's food is crazy in a mofucker. As much as I love my man Grego, I wouldn't think of doing shit like that, and I know he is fucking with that bitch Trish and she's saying her ass is pregnant by him. She say..." Grego cut her off by saying, "Maccadosish is back! Yeah, but I don't have to blurt it out, what do I know about womens emotions, nothing. I have no right to make a judgment, us, men have our issues too!" Something is going on in that supersize brain of E-Tar, and Grego knew it was about them and not me, and to be totally honest, I think we all know the business, because now,

Grego is the bad guy here. I recognized that the discussion was over for the time being, thanks to Q-Loc, his suggestion undoing what they'd just said. He said quietly, "You can't break someone's heart unless they hand it over." He blew out breath, shook his head and said, "T-Mac, man I know you need to hit this weed love one!" Well, all the fixated went back to my attention, Q-Loc said, "The point is, I don't want anybody in here to get hurt either, but I didn't exactly make up that shit you are talking about E-Tar, a top priority."

I was still thinking about Jeanette's phone call as I hit the chronic weed, and I was sipping a drink of Hennessy with apple juice in ice. Dever Fever and Pooh who are mad at each other, said. "Uh-huh, I see your sexy ass has that bitch Jeanette going crazy over you T-Mac", I'm just thinking how appropriate that line Dever Fever said, then she added, "What the hell T- Mac! Maybe just one little kiss wouldn't hurt". Speaking for herself, yeah. I couldn't stop looking at her mouth, her lips were a perfect shape for kissing, and right now they were parted about like the letter "O" which was so damn sexy, I forgot to breathe. It was her lips, but all I saw was Shimin's face there as I drifted closer to her, those glasses would get in the way so that would keep us from getting into full lip-lock mode, Dever Fever voice softened, "Yes, T-Mac babe, kiss me, kiss me!" She giggled, then I said, "No! Dever Fever, I can't do it." "I was considering the last discussion we had, and she is fucking with my love one, Pooh". She said, "How lame you made it sound T-Mac." She glanced up, "T-Mac what do you mean?" I nearly got lost admiring the beauty of her face, "I'm sure I would be a disappointment to you Dever Fever", her lips pushed back in place. "T-Mac, you're probably right. It's a crazy idea anyway, you and me. We'd drive each other nuts like what you're doing to poor Jeanette! Man, women came together big time huh!"

That was the moment when I faced the sorry truth! She said, poor Jeanette, hell, what about, poor T-Mac? I'm the one who almost ate the bloody spaghetti for God's sake. All I come up with was a bunch of statistics that would fit very well in my life of insurance application of crazy women in my life and one coach. A player in love should be able to do better than that. Hell, when a player is in love, he's not a player, he's a guy, that's all. Until recently, that seemed about right to me. Man, the spot is rolling today. Damn! Jeanette and April are here, I ignored her but she called my name again, this time her tone is better so I turned and faced her. "Whassup! Jeanette." She rolled her eyes, maybe because she was smiling, her eyes made an expression to draw me in or drain me off completely. She was more beautiful today than she's ever been, she had jeans and boots on, a blueberry sweatshirt with the word "I love u!" across the front tag in red, bold letters, her long legs and short torso, her long hair in a single braid, she said, "T-Mac! I'd never leave you." Sounds like Jeanette had fallen in love, she falls in love too easily. I suppose, me too but not with her. Shimin is all I'm thinking, the only reason I'm seeing her today is for her ass to not pop up here tomorrow because Shimin is going to be here with me. My heart desires to be happy with Shimin. We both sat on Jeanette's words. My eyes were on hers, her mouth was open, no word but a slight smile, then she shifted like she was about to say something, then quibble again like she changed her mind, did one of those dismissive hand moves she always do to me had changed. She lost all her friendliness, like the kindness had been sucked out of her heart, I shook my head, she said, "You don't respect my time, T-Mac. I'm here to tell you I'm sorry and I told you before to never say that word because a woman will never want a sorry from a man, you remember me telling you that T-Mac?" "Yes, Jeanette I remember!" She had her purse and bottled water in one hand. Her thoughts were careless, she had to think of something back in her shell to get something figured out, before she say it. A look of apprehension painted on Jeanette's face. With her arms folded, eyes on the ground, for Jeanette and I, ten nerve-wrecking minutes passed by. Jeanette looked at her watch and snapped, "I have to take my medicine!" She reached in her purse and pullout three medicine bottles of pills, she was so busy talking and apologizing, she almost forgot to take her medicines. I wiped the stress sweats away from my eyes, I was thinking this is the first time I saw her taking her pills, I feel sorry for her, I just... I just... wanted to kiss her and now I wanted to put my hands around her throat. I had plenty of opportunities too, I clenched my jaw, gritted my teeth, nothing was more salvageable than my thoughts. I couldn't tell if she wants to shoot me or stab me in the throat with a knife. Too many emotions running through us, there's no way to latch on to one, and despite my problems and disposition, I smiled at her.

I remember my promise, to make her happy for her dying wish, I will love her, and for me to look out for her daughters when she passes away.

A thousand questions, what if she's lying to me about dying? I ran my hand over my head, I had that undying love for Jeanette in my eyes, that love that longs my heart or does she have all the power to emasculate me? When a woman falls in love with you, she has a brand new heart. When she falls out of love, the same way when you know she's not in love with you, it hurts like hell. I know Gigi had me for years crying for her love, but the crazy shit is when she come back, I don't care what she did when she was gone, I just want to love her back.

Well, not before I had another payday lined up or tomorrow with Shimin, my frown eased up into one big ambiguous smile. She moved to me, her sweet scent going my way, Jeanette tiptoed and kissed me on the lips, her slender tongue darted into my mouth and she grabbed my ass. She wiped her lipstick off my mouth when she told me she loves me and hugged me. Her body had soft touches, I remember so well, I could memorize from front to back and still be the man living lower than the soles of my shoes. I backed down. I didn't like the way Jeanette is coming at me, she loves me but did some shit like that bloody food. It keeps popping up in my head, she was wrong and she knows it. I'm still pissed! My livelihood was on the line. A new, unreadable emotion flooded her eyes, she said, "Are you coming home tonight, T-Mac?" She was born in a silver spoon world. That shit hit me hard, caught me off guard. "Dammit, Jeanette! You should know." She stopped me. "Be a man, T-Mac! Tell me what you're saying." "Jeanette, this isn't about me. You're the one with the bullshit." I have a problem with how to tell her that I'm not in love with her. Because it hurts! My throat tightened from the memories were too much to bear, things I didn't want to be reminded.

Bloody spaghetti, the thoughts of it keeps ringing through my mind. Damn, what would you do if you were a player? Go home with Jeanette tonight or stay at the spot and wait for Shimin to come tomorrow? With a taste of bitterness on my mind, it got all sweeter by the thought of Shimin coming by. What the hell did I just do? If you guessed it right, I took my ass to Jeanette's house to fuck the shit out of her so she won't fuck up my day with Shimin tomorrow.

You know, when a woman comes with her sex appeal and says she's sorry, which is something she never do (she doesn't want a sorry), sometimes life is cold when you are caught up at a red light with hope and old relationships that you startled through your mind and hoping for the best. But, the thought of what my father used to say, "It's better to be surprised than disappointed." Now, I'm lying here looking at Jeanette and all I can see is the face of Shimin. Wow! Would Jeanette be disappointed knowing I had thoughts of Shimin and not her? Well, I guess I'm surprised that she can soften my heart. Hell, I'm the one who almost ate the bloody spaghetti if it wasn't for the kids.

Well, you know me, with that thought in mind, I had to come up with something to tell Jeanette any reason because I want to go back to Dever fever's house. Jeanette said, "Are you coming back tonight baby?" I said, "Well Jeanette, you know how the spot is, so baby I can't give you that answer, but I will call you and let you know what's going on."

"Oh, hell. Look who's back?" Grego said, "Macadosish is back! Mac, it looked like Jeanette came over here to kick your ass. I'm glad you decided to go over her house and pay her a visit. Hell, I'm not even going to ask what went down, but I'm glad to see Mac is back!" Well, you know when you think you are at a red light and then the light turns green right in front of your face. Stephon startled us with an alert that One Time is hitting a black, if you don't know what I mean, Stephon is the doorman at the spot. Stephon said, "Damn, the motherfucking pigs have been riding by all day and all night stopping in front of the spot. Grego said, "Hell, who gives a damn Stephon, if those mofuckers ain't runnig in our door then we don't give a fuck about what they have going on outside." There was a moment of silence in the spot for a minute, but hell, I guess we are all scared but it's funny how circumstances turn out to become a laughing moment. What Grego just said and Dever Fever also said, "Hell, Mac you have to go give Jeanette some dick, huh. Looked like she came over here to cut off your dick and fuck up some bitches." We all laughed, but I came to quick halt because tonight, the spot is rolling.

Man, it's funny what people would do to get a crack hit. Tango said, "Man, y'all need to be careful and shut down the spot tonight cause I feel like they are about to raid somebody!" "Hell, Tango!", Grego said "if we shut down every time the police come around, we ain't going to make money!" Q-Loc said, "We ain't going to give you a crack hit for telling us that shit!" Tango said, "Fuck you motherfucker! Hurry up, give me a dub so I can get the hell out of here! But I ain't playing motherfucker, y'all got the best dope in San Diego, I don't want to see you all go to jail." Grego said, "What are you talking about that jail shit, Tango? Are you working with the police or something?" I said, "Tango, where did you get those twenty dollars? You got that from the police or something?" Tango said, "You brothers got me fucked up. Stephon, hurry up and open this door so I can get out of here." To me, my thoughts are rumbling caged up like a prisoner with the thoughts of disbelief because the look Tango had on his face seems more concern like there was betrayal, not like the usual Tango who comes over here. Well, let me tell you a little something about Tango, he used to be a San Diego Golden Glove, he came to the spot bobbing and weaving side to side telling his stories, that's why everybody calls him Tango. Man, it brings a thought to my mind far away from here, then it slice that I'm in right now. All of the love that I had for running and Tango had for boxing, all of the sudden we lost the love and hurt feelings started flashing through my mind of Gigi' face buttering up from the sun, sitting there at my track and field event blowing kisses, saying "Baby win, wind for me. Baby win!"

Man, with the thought of love and betrayal and what's new, I need to cheer my heart up and leave behind what's in the past and leading forward into tomorrow to have a good day with Shimin. She takes away all the hurt feelings of my past experience with my ex-girlfriends. Dever Fever said, "Hell, Mac, you know that phone is for you." With the thought of Dever Fever saying that puts a hard rock pain to my stomach knowing it's Jeanette on the other line, it seems like a never ending call that it took me a long while to go there and pick up the phone thinking what the hell am I going to say to her. My thoughts have nothing good to say, hell, I'm going to tell Jeanette to not mess up my day with Shimin tomorrow.

"Hello", I said. My mind froze with the softest voice I could remember, the Shimin said, "Hey T-Mac, what took you so long to come to the phone?" With the enthusiasm and excitement in my voice, I said "Hey Shimin, what's going on home girl? Are you still coming over tomorrow?" "Yes T-Mac," Shimin said, "That's why I'm calling you to ask what time you are going to pick me up in the morning? If you don't mind, I have a couple of home girls who would love to come too."

"Yes, Shimin!" I said, "so what time do you want me to pick you up?"

"You know my dad is a police officer, so I will give you a call when he leaves for work."

"Okay Shimin, that sounds cool, so make sure you call me in the morning when he leaves."

"Man, my nigga!" I said, "Guess who I was on the phone with my nigga? It was Shimin, you know? The one I brought over here, the one I met on the mall. I know all of you were telling me that this fine bitch ain't going to call me back, well niggas, let me tell you this; she said she's coming over here tomorrow and she's bringing some home girls! Which one of you ugly niggas owes me some pimpin fees?" The Mac time Grammy winner has been known to infiltrate, I thought about it, I couldn't even hold the phone when Shimin was on the line.

There were a lot of people and homies who thought that I couldn't do it. I just blurted out, "I love you guys!"

I was an international player before, I remember when I lost my mind, cheesy relationships and my ex-relationship, that's right! I need to stop snooping. Insecurities will kill a relationship faster than anything else. The best relationship advice I've ever got is from Eazy-E's song "Easy does it". Eric White's advice impacted the way I approach romantic relationship, that I deserve a lot more and that's why Shimin will be here at the dope spot the day after today. My cousins will be getting their clowning on, yes, on me, and make up and entertainers by Pantomime common situations or actions in exaggerated or ridiculous fashion by tumbling comedy about Shimin's friends.

Q-Loc said, "Fine ass bitches like Shimin always have ugly friends." The living got full of laughter, then Dever fever said, "Q-Loco! What did you just say?" She comes from the kitchen to the living room snacking on a bunch of bananas, she dragged from the kitchen laughing about Q-Loc's joke.

Thinking about better times must have been out of my mind, so I'm running back to tell you, all I'm after is a life full of laughter, as long as I'm laughing with them, I'm thinking that all that matters is love ever after. The living room displays of humor all through the night.

I love my family. If someone were to harm my family,

or friends or someone that I love, I would eat them alive even if I might end up in a correctional facility, detention center, jail, penitentiary or prison. Dever fever said, "You guys are talking about Shimin's friends, I'm the finest bitch around!" We laughed so hard.

Then I made my way to my bedroom, I know Shimin will be making her way to my bedroom. Tomorrow is going to be a special day so I started to pray, I said, "Lord, if you are real, I need a sweet little something like Shimin sliding into my world. Amen." But I'm tired of talking so I went to bed. I said to myself that I was having a bad dream about Jeanette and she was telling me, "I believe it was a sign, do you love me in the way I see you T-Mac?" I couldn't believe the shit Jeanette was saying with the bloody menstruation in my spaghetti. The thought, images and sensation stays in my mind. I had a recurrent dream about falling from great height and I wake up from my dream. Jeanette had a voodoo curse on me, I couldn't wake up. I find myself walking down a dark, weary hallway, at the end of the hallway, I can hear Kiana's voice calling my name, "T-Mac…" then I wake up from my dream to see Kiana standing over in my bed. "Hey Kiana," I said, "What's up T- Mac?" Kiana said, "So what do you have on your agenda for the day?" All I can do is look at her and I am so worried that she knows something abut Shimin coming over here today that she's not telling me about. I said, "Jeanette told you to come over here to spy on me like a secret agent? Well, Kiana I have a lot of shit to do today." Then Kiana said, "Like that bitch Shimin, Mac?" "Kiana! What the fuck are you talking about?" Kiana said, "T-Mac, San Diego is a very small place, everybody knows everybody's business. If you let me and my home girls stay on the spot, I won't tell my mom about you, and we want McDonald's too." I said, "Hell yeah, Kiana, you got that! But who spilled the beans on me?" Her face turned into a funny laughing gester but the bloody smile across her face is a contradiction. "Mac, haven't you ever heard of the power I have over people? And I'm not telling you anything, Mac!" Kiana said. It was the earliest use of spilling the beans on me and Kiana is blackmailing me. Hell, it's just McDonalds, I can go for a Big Mac burger too.

Shimin finally called and I looked at the clock, it is 9:30 A.M. "So, Shimin, did your dad leave for work already because I don't want to come over and he will put his hands on me?" Shimin said, "My dad is not going to do that," then I cut her off, I said, "Shimin remember what your dad said, what are those thugs doing in front of my house?" "Well T-Mac, he won't be off work until 6:00 this evening so I want you to bring me and my home girls back by 4:00. Is that cool, T-Mac?" she said. "Yes Shimin, so what time do you want me to pick you up?" I asked. Then she answered, "We are here waiting for you now."

I was startled by Dever fever standing by the bedroom door saying something to me. I have a feeling that Dever fever is up to something, her body languge is sending sexual gestures to me, rocking her hips side by side with her hands on her waist and she laid it down on me. "T-Mac!" she said, "You know I'm still a sexy bitch and if I weren't pregnant, I will so in there and fuck the shit out of your ass. I'm not playing with you T-Mac, so now tell me that I'm still a sexy bitch." So I said, "Well Dver fever, I know about the bitch part but you look like you ate a big pumpkin belly pie standing there with all the crumbs around your mouth. Before I tell you you're sexy, I want to know if you can sneak me out to Kiana because she's blackmailing me for some McDonalds." She was laughing out loud and swinging around and shaking her ass while singing a song then said, "You can get me big mac too since I can't eat your ass. By the way, Mac, better let them bitches know I'm the Queen Bee in this house!" I said with a cool gesture, "You got that Dever fever."

So I went outside to warm up Dollar. While I'm sitting in my car, my car phone rang, "Hey baby," a soft voice said, "You were T-Mac the Tiger last night. I cooked you breakfast this morning, are you going to come and eat?" I said, "Jeanette, I have to go to L.A for an emergency so I won't be back until later tonight." She said, "Okay baby, be careful." Wow! I hope she believed that, well who gives a fuck anyway. With a fire ass like Shimin, she can walk on the door and see me pounding that ass. Man, today the streets look quite, there's something spooky about this, I don't see any drug pusher, kart pusher and crack heads in Oceanview Blvd. As soon as I hit the corner on Imperial Highway, I can see a group of undercover cops getting suited so I hurried up and turned down my monster sounds playing Run DMC's "Rock the bells". All the cops looked over to me as I passed by. I immediately phone Grego, "Grego," I said, "There's a bunch of pigs around the cornergetting suited and booked so tell Stephon to keep his head up and lock out the door." Greg always speak in a soft beat voice, you would have to do something really wrong for him to raise his voice. He said in a llam, cool voice, "All right Macadosish, you do good in looking out. Oh, by the way T-Mac, Kiana is sitting over there with all her home girls and said don't forget her McDonalds." I said, "Okay Grego."

I'm gone as I approached Shimin's house, I can see she's playing with one of her friends outside, ready to go. Man, I can't wait until I get back to the spot because last night they were laughing, talking about fine ass bitches always have ugly girlfriends but all of Shimin's friends are fine as hell! So, they all jumped in and headed to McDonalds on the way. It was a car full of girls giggling and laughing in the conversation they were having.

"Hello, may I take your order?" I was sitting back, smoking some cigarettes, then I coughed some smoke and said, "Give me ten of everything on the menu", and the voice in the speaker said, "Could you repeat that order?" "I said ten of everything on the menu." Then she said, "Well Sir, you need to come in for that order." I said, "Damn, all right I'll be there."

On the way back to the spot, I noticed that the pigs are still sitting in the same spot but now in full uniform and all eyes on me. Then Shimin said, "Hey, those are all my daddy's friends over there." Man, there are fifteen pigs over there, I hope their ass will hit the castle and don't hit our ass.

I wish you could see the look on my cousin's faces when they saw how fine they all are. We had the dope spot cracking today, smoking big weed, playing loud music, eating McDonalds and drinking Hennessey. Even Kiana's friends are fine. Grego jumped from his chair pointing his hand and stomping his feet saying "There they go, there they go!" real loud, so me and Todd grabbed the plate of dope on the table, I snatched it from his hands, ran to the bathroom and flushed it down the toilet. And as I am looking around the room, the look on all the girls' faces reminded me of Zelda and my cousin Q- Loc sitting back watching "Good Fellas" but this is not a movie, we were the good fellas living the life. While Shimin was screaming that her father is going to kill him if he got wind of her hanging out with thugs and in a dope spot, of all places.

April, Myesha, Etar, Trish, Dever fever, Kiana and all of her girlfriends were all screaming, it was pure chaos. Still going through with all of the commotion, I can hear the glass shattering from the outside. All of this was going on while my hands are I the toilet dumping the dope. Neat thing. Then I heard the police yelling "Get down everybody! Get your hands up and get down on the ground!" And while they were getting the people in the living room, that gave me a brief minute to creep through the hallway to the back room.

I was going to jump out the window, when I finally did arrive to the back room window, I was greeted by Todd and Grego, they also were going to jump out the window so I started yelling at them to hurry up and jump already. In my mind I was thinking, look at these two fools just standing there looking like two mannequins. I looked over their shoulders to see this ninja standing there. I haven't ever seen this kind of shit before so he instructed us to lay down on the bed, and at that exact moment, it was time to resume and just abide by the instructions of the officer dressed like a ninja.

As I landed on the bed, I could hear the voices of Bob and Q-Loc, they were talking shit while being cuffed in the other room. This shit is wild and going down, I couldn't believe how everything go down so I started to look around and noticed that the ninja cop was gone. I looked at Grego and Todd, so I thought to myself, I am going to get up of the bed and try to find a way out but a voice yelled out from the living room telling us to get back down on the bed. "We have you tracked, we can see you through the walls." So, they finally made their way back to the room where me, Grego and Todd were in, but they walked in, it was like a scene out of a movie. These cops were dressed in all black from head to toe and the guns that they have are pointing at us, it was nothing like I had seen before.

So, once they got everybody detained, the ninjas called for the other cops to come in and just like a thief in the night, the ninjas disappeared. And what do you know about the luck that we have today, because the cops that came in next were friends of Shimin's dad. The day couldn't get any worse.

Now, we are all outside, there is like twenty of us sitting in the front yard while he dad's buddies searched the house. I watched while all of the cops that were there yelled at Shimin for being there, they couldn't believe that she was even there and if her dad knows about it. She tried to explain that she and her friends were just socializing and eating McDonalds. So, finally after about an hour of searching the spot, they came out empty-handed, they couldn't find any drugs and guns but what they did find was some weed and some of our military bullets that no one is even supposed to have.

So now, they were asking how we got a hold of those kinds of bullets. Then, the head sergeant ordered the officers to uncuff all of the ladies but only after they have been patted down. They took all of the guys down to the station, I mean they interrogated the fuck out of everybody but team stayed loyal and solid and without any evidence, they don't have a case so they had to let us go.

Now, things at the spot just went downhill. Dever fever was spooked, I mean I understand she didn't want to lose her child so it pushed us out of the street corner and that was a sure key for disaster because what do you know? Word travelled around town fast that our million dollars spot was shut down and we were out curb serving. So a couple of dudes tried to press us and somehow I wound up being arrested on three attempted murder charges. I sat in the country for a year while fighting these charges but they did find out that they pulled weapons on me first. I mean, I just couldn't believe how this whole situation got so blown up that we made it to the front page of the San Diego paper.

One day, the cops came to me and said that I have a visitor. In my mind, I thought it was Jeanette but it was a lawyer from a law firm in San Francisco saying he knew me. But this whole situation was just crazy because he is not just an ordinary lawyer, he is the owner of the firm and you would never believe our connection. And while all of this is going on, the only thought running in my mind was that day when I was at Camp Bloomfield sitting on top of the water tower, looking down on the beach the day I left and retired my Goodwill track shoes with all of my dreams of doing sports. But, when Philip mentioned the time that Ronald Regan, in one of my track meets, said how proud he is of my achievements is what drove him to come down and help but in return, I have to give up my third place bronze medal that I won. I agreed and that's why I only had to do a year of country time.

He dropped off a lot of things, dropped and thrown out, and to this day, he still has my broze medal in his office. I know you are wondering why this medal meant so much and it's because we did something in the state finals that wasn't heard of before, dropped the hand off and still ended up placing third place.

While I was doing my time, me and Jeanette talked a lot and she keeps on telling me that she's going to hold on to me and she will not die until I got home. The girl is crazy and all the way gone insane, she doesn't make any sense anymore. The whole time she is talking about that crazy talk, all I could think of was how I never got the chance to fuck Shimin.

Now, upon the dawn of my release, my brother KT came to pick me up in Dallas. I went smooth to my brother in the police parking lot. I was gone for a motherfucking year, can you tell me who fucked off my car Dollar like this? It was a fucked bucket now, not even worth 5 cents. I looked over at my older brother with his head hanging low. Then, we went straight to Jeanette's house. When I stepped inside the front door, I felt chills running through my whole body, it was a different kind of feeling, not an ounce of joy or happiness to finally be able to see me after being gone for this past year. I was greeted with sadness from Sheran, Apirl, Keana and Myesha. I don't nderstand what is going on, so you know me, being the Mac, I started cracking jokes trying to get a smile but they still have stone faces in front of me. Then, I heard Jeanette's voice from the back room saying, "Is that my baby in there?" So I started to walk off with my cool guy attitude like, yes it is! But, Sharon caught me by my arm and said, "Mac, since you have been gone, my mom changed a lot and I don't want it to catch you off guard but my mom is not the same person you and I knew. She stopped going to chemo, she lost a lot of weight and her hair." I'm trying to play it cool like, "come on Sharon, that's my girl, I can handle it." As soon as I entered the bedroom, my heart seemed to jump up and out of my chest that it took my breath away. I just turned around, walked back to the living room and put my hands over my eyes and said, "I need a mother fucking drink." That's not my girl, not my Jeanette. Damn, cancer took her down when I thought she was just lying to me about dying but now I found out that she's telling the truth.

While taking back a couple of shots, I finally got my composure back so that I could go and face her. I found the courage to walk back to her room. When I got there, I sat in a seat that was by her bed side and I grabbed her hand. She said, "Please be quite T-Mac, I want you to make a promise to me to always be a part of my daughters' lives." I feel like it was taking all the energy and strength that she had to get me to understand what was on her heart and her last wish is for me to always remain in her daughters' lives and I told her that she could count on me. Then she went on and said that she asked my lawyer if I could stay here because I had to go back to L.A and he said no because San Diego country didn't want me around there. So I said my goodbyes as I headed off to my probation officer and that very next day when I was in Long Beach in my probation officer's office, I got call from my uncle Tank. He said, "Mac, are you sitting down?" It threw me off so I said, "Huh?". Then Uncle Tank said, "I have some bad news for you. Jeanette just passed away this morning."

Damn, at that moment, it was a lot of mixed emotions racing through me; happiness, sadness, love and joy because it felt like her spirit was there in the office with me and the feeling that she was in heaven and not here living in pain and suffering anymore. It was a blessing that my probation officer gave me a pass so that I could attend Jeanette's funeral. Somehow, I know that it was Jeanette who touched my probation officer's heart so I could get the pass to go because she ended up losing her job because of that and that's how I know it was Jeanette's spirit.

As time goes on, I get a call from Robert, he said that Eazy E wanted to meet the crew, so here I am, an official member of Ruthless Records. And now, things are about to warm up with the real ruthless records scandal with this whole WWA movie and how they patronized Mister Eric Wright, better known as Eazy E. But damn, when things just start to get better, something always comes along to fuck things up. Here, for the first time coming of the Ruthless Record, it is also the introduction of Bone Thugs and Harmony with Ruthless Records and the 7th sign with Bizzy Bone and CNO SouldJahz with Ackileer.

King G, that's a whole nother story. I was on the phone with my son, Jack the Mogul, a platinum award winning artist, then King G showed up in sight. He was one of the original homies from the CNO click when they started. The first time AC Killer recorded a song was on his computer and from then on, Heinz and AC Killer took off with music ever since they found out they could do productions on their own. Back then, King G's name was G Nyce, the name he got when he was first put on in his first neighborhood, West Bang. When Big Syke from the Outlawz/THUG LIFE first met G Nyce, he pulled him out of his first neighborhood and put him on his, IVC, the only crip neighborhood in Inglewood. He switched his name to Baby G and every one in the hood new him as that. Thing was, he had a public access show in the Valley called On Da Real and everyone their new him as King G. He's got a lot of stories with all the camps, known with rapping and directing movies, but what I thought was interesting about him was how he worked as head of security for Michael Jackson on his 45th birthday at Neverland Ranch. Him and Mike Tyson walked Michael Jackson on stage while Ryan Seacrest was pissed at MJ for postponing his performance on live radio for almost a hour long. He got songs with 16--time Grammy award winner David Bantor, the Long Beach crew rolling with Snoop Dogg and the Doggpound (Blacc Jesus), and other producers/artists around the way. He got stories with everyone from Scarlett Johansen, Pink, Chris Tucker, Van Damme, T.I., Mopreme Shakur and several others. He also has a bunch of movies made under his belt like "Rocks, Paper, Scissors", "Last Thug Standing", "Getaway Robber", "Watts: City Schemers", "Big Syke: Immortal" and unseen footage with 2Pac Shakur. His films, songs and writings have received acclaim, making him a real G doing the craft properly. I figured he was the only guy I could trust for telling the true story of Eazy E. I hollered at him and now we have a theatrical distribution deal in the works for the infamous upcoming film Eazy Duz It which tells the true story of my man, my boss, Eric Wright.

The End

This is an introduction to my life's events. All the things are all facts and no fiction. Names have been changed to protect people's identity. I hope you enjoy my book.

Thank you very much.

Printed in the United States
By Bookmasters